MARK TWAIN in the MOVIES

MARK TWAIN

in the

MOVIES

A Meditation with Pictures
by John Seelye

THE VIKING PRESS   NEW YORK

First published in 1977 by The Viking Press
625 Madison Avenue, New York, N.Y. 10022
Published simultaneously in Canada by
Penguin Books Canada Limited

LIBRARY OF CONGRESS CATALOGING IN PUBLICATION DATA
Seelye, John D
    Mark Twain in the movies.
    1. Clemens, Samuel Langhorne, 1835–1910.
    2. Authors, American—19th century—Biography.
    3. Clemens, Samuel Langhorne, 1835–1910—Portraits,
    etc. 4. Authors, American—19th century—Portraits.
    I. Title.
    PS1331.S37 818'.4'09 [B] 77–21472
    ISBN 0–670–45830–9

Printed in the United States of America
Set in VIP Garamond

ACKNOWLEDGMENTS: Harper & Row, Publishers, Inc.: From *Mark Twain: A Biography*, Volumes I–IV, by Albert Bigelow Paine. Copyright 1912 by Harper & Row, Publishers, Inc.; renewed 1940 by Dora L. Paine. Reprinted by permission of Harper & Row, Publishers, Inc. University of Oklahoma Press: From *Enchantment: A Little Girl's Friendship with Mark Twain* by Dorothy Quick. Copyright © 1961 by the University of Oklahoma Press.

PICTURE CREDITS: Except where designated below, all pictorial matter appears here through the courtesy of the Mark Twain Papers, The Bancroft Library, University of California, Berkeley.
    Henderson, *Mark Twain:* 2, 18, 19, 65 right. Quick, *Enchantment:* 125, 126. Wallace, *Mark Twain and The Happy Island:* 80, 91, 96–98, 105, 111–13, 138 both, 149. Library of Congress: 67–69, 109 right. Mark Twain Memorial, Hartford, Conn.: 6, 20, 25, 32, 35, 40–44, 59, 70, 71, 72 right, 75, 88, 93 left. Wadsworth Atheneum, Hartford, Ella Gallup Sumner and Mary Catlin Sumner Collection: 64. Wilson Library, University of North Carolina, Chapel Hill, N.C.: 7–9, 52, 72 left.
    The sequence of pictures from the silent film, "Mark Twain at Stormfield," which appears on pages 19–83, was made possible through the cooperation and courtesy of the Mark Twain Memorial.

CONTENTS

It was a pretty sight to see him teaching his little girl friends to play, and encouraging them by letting them beat him.

—Elizabeth Wallace, *Mark Twain and The Happy Island*

Mark Two

?

There always have been two Mark Twains, and there probably always will be, for duality seems to be intrinsic to the man and his work. We may distinguish at the start the difference between Mark Twain and Samuel Langhorne Clemens, a subject on which more than one book has been written, but in terms of our own point of view, and by *our* I mean the general, popular viewpoint, the distinction is not so clear. Therefore there now exists a different pair of twins, the Mark Twain of the marketplace and he of the academy. Unlike most of his contemporaries—William Dean Howells especially (and undeservedly)—Mark Twain continues to enjoy a wide popularity, and is still read by a large number of Americans. His re-creation by Hal Holbrook undoubtedly broadened that audience considerably, and it also served to remind us that the old man's quips are still very timely, that his jokes are still funny. At the same time, the work of the editors of Mark Twain's unpublished manuscripts, the most of them written during his old age, reveals an unhumorous side, a dark, pessimistic dimension suggesting that the origins of laughter are indeed complex. We may doubt, moreover, that many general readers have availed themselves of the texts carefully prepared by Frederick Anderson, John Tuckey, William Gibson, and others, and may rest fairly certain that it is the "other" Mark Twain, the popular entertainer familiar to his contemporaries, who continues to dominate the public consciousness.

Perhaps one of the reasons why Mark Twain continues to live as a writer is that no one has come along to replace him. There was Will Rogers, but Rogers never transcended his role as stand-up comedian, never wrote an undeniable masterpiece like *The Adventures of Huckleberry Finn*. Mark Twain did, and in that book as in so much else he wrote and said, he put forth the rudiments of the modern American consciousness, statements so powerful they make the wit and wisdom of Will Rogers shrink to the size and shape of a wizened midget. Hemingway said that modern American literature begins with *Huckleberry Finn,* but he was stating only half the story. If *the* American dilemma is the uneasy and often tragic relationship between black men and white, if *the* American sickness is nostalgia, if *the* American theme is pastoral in coloration (i.e., green) and picaresque in plot, if *the* secret of American manhood is perpetual boyhood, even to the ultimate social bond, then *Huckleberry Finn* is about what we are all about. And in Mark Twain himself we can detect a forecast of the modern condition, for in his gigantic faith in and uneasiness over the millennial, even salvational, role of the Machine, we can read our own apocalyptic conclusions.

Still, the popular sense of Mark Twain seldom includes these darker aspects of the man who was so much a part of the Gilded Age he named. We love him only incidentally for his doubts; we love him because he makes us laugh, because we still sense in him what his contemporaries felt—his massive humanness. His image is our national literary icon, his picture a secular equivalent of a Saint Christopher medal, because like the wading saint he helps us over the hard crossings of life. He mediates for us between not the Christ but the Devil in us all. As a secular saint he is a figure of Wisdom, and it is notable that the image most familiar to us moderns is the old man with the Einstein-like mop of white hair. As Old Man he is a modern version of the court jester, being a licensed fool whose sharp tongue and mocking squint are permitted because we acknowledge the necessity of such saving wisdom. We grant him the luxury of his sarcasm concerning our most hallowed institutions because we cannot ourselves afford it. We laugh with him at the stupidity of the jury system, the venality of Congress, and the imperial tendency of the Presidency, and then we go on supporting those corrupted ideals. We join with him in sighing over the loss of our rural Golden Age, but then we go back to work building an uncertain bridge to an unknown future. And so did he.

This book is written against that strange necessity, not in an adversary manner (though a certain asperity may be detected) but in the manner of a magic-lantern show thrown upon a patterned screen. Written with Mark Twain's popular image in mind, what follows is an attempt to demonstrate the ambivalence of that image—the picture of the white old man hanging in our mental parlors—and it proceeds by playing off text (or meditation) against the amazing variety which that single picture can put forth. As image, that is to say, Mark Twain is as various as the works he wrote, being a public man of numerous roles and a private man of as many more. This book is built on the assumption that we all know and love the public phenomenon we call Mark Twain, and it concludes on a note of acceptance (even insistence) concerning the validity of that image. But it is written (and assembled) with the felt necessity of projecting a counterimage, of delineating the shadow behind the gleaming white silhouette.

What follows are sixteen very brief chapters that attempt to present different aspects of Mark Twain, both in pictures and in the events of his public and private life. No attempt is made to draw a clear and consistent distinction

between Mark Twain and the man who created him, because I believe the line is not at all clear, especially during the last ten years of his life—the chronological frame stressed here. I hope, if anything, to destroy the vestiges of that line, and by so doing to increase rather than reduce the complexity of the creation, Mark Twain, so that when his great white presence flashes again on the screen, our reaction can never again be so simplistic as before. For Mark Twain is, as I suggest below, the Moby Dick of American letters, his very whiteness connoting at the last a horrific void. A problem as complex as any of the puzzle characters created by Henry James, he cannot finally be known by the stare direct, but must be scrutinized in a series of circumventions, like many another ghost best caught out of the corner of one's eye. We may finally remain uncertain as to what we saw, yet the oblique angle will be essential to the vision. It is the sideways slant of humor that can become the painful glance of madness, the both of which are always, whether in Hamlet, King Lear, or Mark Twain, closely allied.

Even as Hal Holbrook was resurrecting the funny Mark Twain, a somewhat less lovable ghost was being conjured up by several scholars, commencing with Justin Kaplan's popular biography and culminating with Hamlin Hill's study, a book to which my own presentation owes a very large debt. Hill picks up where Kaplan leaves off, and in expanding upon the details of Mark Twain's last ten years, the period during which he attained his public sainthood, he demonstrates a demarcation more radical than the distinction Kaplan establishes between Samuel Clemens and his literary persona, a difference that darkens at last into tragedy. Though my own efforts are aimed at creating a unity from this disjunction, mine is a structure that leans very heavily on Hamlin Hill's book, which deserves a much wider audience than it has hitherto had, as I hope my frequent references to it will suggest.

I am indebted also, though in a different way, to the following persons and institutions: to the University of North Carolina for a Kenan Leave which permitted this sortie into what was an unplanned direction; to the Photographic Laboratory of the Wilson Library, Mr. Samuel M. Boone director, and to the labors especially of Bryan Jones, whose own devotion to Mark Twain added an unexpected dimension; to Mr. Frederick Anderson, of the Mark Twain Papers at the University of California, who extended personally and through his staff a number of courtesies, only partly acknowledged in the list of photo credits; to Mr. Frederick Voss, of the National Portrait Gallery, for similar favors; to Mr. Wilson H. Faude, Curator of the Mark Twain Memorial, for having made available among other illustrations the prints from the motion picture of Mark Twain that enliven these pages; and to Professor Bigelow Paine Cushman, who generously responded to my inquiries concerning the photographic career of his grandfather, the biographer of Mark Twain.

But my largest debt, and it is one shared by all of us interested in Mark Twain, is to Miss Isabel V. Lyon, his long-suffering secretary, to whom we owe the extensive record, in diaries and photographs, of his private life during its last decade. Through the agency of others, the diaries were added to the Mark Twain Papers, and provided much of the material used by Hamlin Hill. But only lately, through the graciousness of Miss Lyon's surviving family, was the bulk of her photographs acquired by the Bancroft Library, a sampling of which is reproduced here.

The better part remains, to which the pictures printed in this book serve as an introduction, attesting to yet another talent of a most remarkable person, partner for a time to that most singularly divided personage, Mark Twain.

MARK TWAIN in the MOVIES

Mark Trade

We know our writers by their works and by their pictures, and many Americans know the picture best. Of twentieth-century writers, the grizzly bearded Hemingway, the mustachioed Faulkner, and the tassel-headed Norman Mailer number among the most familiar faces, but when it comes to the writers of an earlier generation, Mark Twain holds the record for half-profile visibility. It is, moreover, the *old* Mark Twain, with his wild puff of white hair and all-season white suit, that is the most familiar image, a prevalence Hal Holbrook at once certified and gave further mileage to, stamping that mischievous visage for good and all upon the popular consciousness. Robert Frost tried hard to displace him, but Mark Twain remains foxy grandpa to us all.

It is fitting, moreover, that the image endures, engendered as it was at the start of this century, for if, as Hemingway claimed, modern American literature begins with a book called *The Adventures of Huckleberry Finn*, then our modern notion of what an author should be starts with a man called Mark Twain. We may date the man in the white flannel (or serge, depending upon the season) suit from about 1907, at the end of forty years of public recognition that began when Mark Twain leapt into national view astride his Calaveras bullfrog in 1865. As a lecturer and then a popular writer of travel books and fiction, Mark Twain (the name, being a trademark, must always be used entire) was never unwilling to post his face in a public place. As American graffito he was from the beginning camera sly, and the first known photograph of the young Clemens is of a brash fifteen-year-old printer's devil holding a compositor's stick that carries his name in banner type. As advertisement for himself, it is a visual trick which turns on the fact that the daguerreotype produces a mirror image,

1

thereby registering the letters SAM as they would appear on the printed page.

To get a true picture of young Clemens we must reverse the image once again.

Duplicity depending upon technology, old and new, it was but the first of Sam's several shticks, including the handlebar mustache that he nourished in the Far West, the flourishes of a man who wishes to be remembered if not entirely known. Late in his life, Mark Twain's shuffling walk was captured in jigtime by the motion-picture camera, perhaps with Edison at the other end, and rumors persist that the Wizard of Menlo Park also caught Mark Twain's drawling voice in wax. But the most enduring personal banner of strange device is the unruly head of hair that became a white blossom triumphing over the snowbank of old age, and as with the earliest image we have of young Sam Clemens, we owe the White Old Man to not the moving but the still camera, a modern marvel of which Mark Twain made good use.

He was fond of recalling aloud and in print that he was born the year Halley's Comet flashed across the sky, predicting he would depart when the comet returned—as indeed he did. But 1835 was also the year in which Louis Jacques Mandé Daguerre accidentally discovered the alchemical effect of mercury vapor upon iodide of silver, a wedding of Mercury and Diana which would prove not only a powerful mythic match but a horoscope for the infant born in Florida, Missouri. And as Mark Twain lay dying in 1910, D. W. Griffith went west with Mary Pickford and Billy Bitzer to make his first motion pictures in California. While Halley's Comet sailed through its perihelion once again the first stars were being born of an incredible galaxy that would make a Los Angeles suburb holy ground, and the passing of Mark Twain was an integral part of that cosmic advent. Having gained his first fame in (and by means of) California, Mark Twain left the place in 1868, not to return, but he was and would always remain California's child, even after he had got rid of the unwieldy sobriquet, "The Wild Humorist of the Pacific Slope." There are memorials to him in Missouri and Connecticut, but perhaps the greatest monument of all is Hollywood, a place where he never was but will always remain.

At about the same time that he had his moving picture taken Mark Twain sold the movie rights to *The Prince and the Pauper* to Edison—for $150—but it was not in these minor matters that he helped make the way straight for Babylon. It was, rather, a personal quality, Mark Twain's mixture of charisma and chutzpah that we may equate with modern stardom, an equation made easier by the pictorial record and by the facts of his life. Even if he had never been caught coming down the path in a Chaplinesque gait, Mark Twain would have remained the original Kineman, for he was *homo movens* personified—Man in Motion. From his first travel books to his last unfinished fantasies about voyages into final darkness, Mark Twain took his materials from real or imagined journeys, and his greatest work of fiction concerns a raft floating down the Mississippi. Time travel too was his convention, from the Connecticut Yankee's voyage to medieval England to Mark Twain's own personal recovery of lost times, *Life on the Mississippi*.

As a traveler Mark Twain was nothing if not commercial, and many of his best-known works were sold by subscription, high-pressure door-to-door sales that guaranteed a certain margin of profit even before the book went into production. The book agent's burden was lightened by having his product weighted down with pictures and begauded with gilt decorations, resulting in objects designed to be placed in the very parlors Mark Twain ridiculed in "The House Beautiful" (*Life on the Mississippi*), his *Innocents Abroad* being an American Pilgrim's Progress packaged to be placed next to the one by Bunyan. They were late-nineteenth-century versions of what are today called coffee-table books, and because of the preponderance of pictures, a good number being of Mark Twain himself—who was the leading character in his travel writings—the author enjoyed a recognition factor to be envied by modern writers, whose faces are tossed away with the dust jacket.

By 1883 Mark Twain was so universally recognizable that he could, in *Life on the Mississippi*, turn a little joke on himself by attempting to travel down the great river incognito—with predictable results. Having introduced himself to the pilot as a stranger to the great river, Mark Twain is drawn into a long, leg-pulling dialogue about dredging for alligators, only to discover that the pilot knew who he was all along. The masquerade, like many episodes in his travel books, was a pure fiction, but it *might* have happened, and in any event the artist helped drive the lesson of the anecdote home.

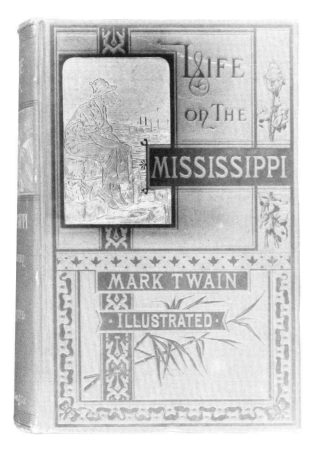

5¢

MARK TWAIN

SUMATRA WRAPPER

Mark Twain

KNOWN TO EVERYONE - LIKED BY ALL

By 1883 Mark Twain had registered his name as a trademark, thereby stamping his writings as products as well as works, and he was not unwilling to rent his face out for profit too. His features appeared on cigar boxes,

tobacco premiums,

COMING !

cigarette coupons,

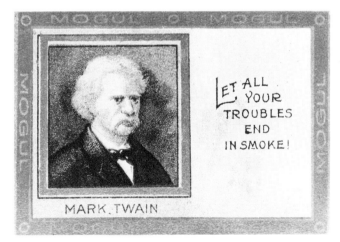

LET ALL YOUR TROUBLES END IN SMOKE!

MARK TWAIN

11

and on advertising matter in general.

Mark Twain.

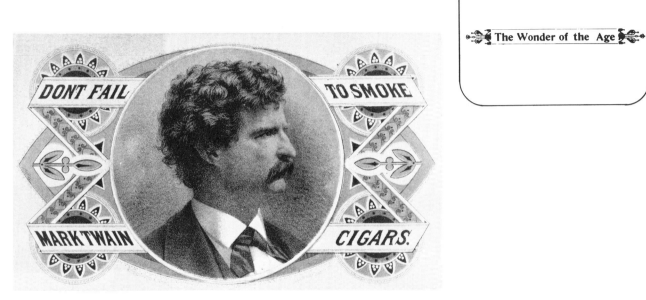

DONT FAIL TO SMOKE

MARK TWAIN CIGARS.

The Wonder of the Age

Before his death Mark Twain's face
had reached the kind of currency our Presidents attain only *after* they die,

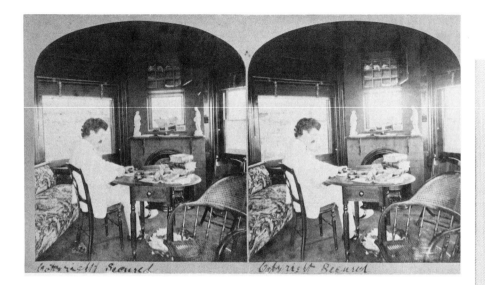

Copyright Secured   Copyright Secured

Famous Authors
(Men)

E. F. Harkins

14

and it is obvious that the Americans who loved Mark Twain were desirous of looking upon him as well. This hawking of his aquiline profile is singular in the annals of American literature, for though the hairy faces of the Fireside Poets, Longfellow and Whittier, were as familiar to the family circle as the Smith Brothers, Mark Twain made sure that his hirsute image appeared in both the bookstore *and* the pharmacy. Wherever paper or tobacco was sold, there was Mark Twain, alongside the stationery and next to Lydia Pinkham.

Not even the most popular writers of today share Mark Twain's iconographic popularity, and to find a reasonable facsimile we have to turn to show business and sports—which as a business is mostly show—a fact further certifying Mark Twain's ascendancy as a star of paramount magnitude. Where fellow writers like Henry James and William Dean Howells occasionally allowed their faces to appear outside the study door, gracing an article in some literary magazine, as early as 1874 Mark Twain's fans could peer in at him working at his desk, through their stereoscopes, bringing him into their homes in three dimensions and into the company of such wonders of the ancient and modern worlds as the Pyramids of Egypt and the Flatiron Building. When, therefore, a book was published in 1901 called *Famous Authors (Men)*, the most famous of all appeared on the cover in a nest of flowers, having become by then something of a parlor artifact himself. "The average American loves his family," said Thomas Alva Edison about this time. "If he has any love left over for some other person, he generally selects Mark Twain." Naturally, as with light bulbs, gramophone records, and moving pictures, the average American was willing to pay for that privilege.

EDISON'S ● MARVELOUS

MAGNISCOPE

Showing Moving Pictures.

Saint Mark

Nothing is calculated to please a man more than the things said about him after he dies, and something of the veneration Americans felt for Mark Twain is suggested by the title of William Dean Howells's eulogizing memoir, *My Mark Twain.* Howells had many friends among the literati, but we could hardly imagine such a chummy title cozying up to the likes of Henry James. In announcing the closeness of his relationship, Howells was appealing to readers who shared his feelings and wished to participate vicariously in the intimate moments shared with the man he called Clemens—because, as he explained, the other name seemed "to mask him from my personal sense." But by separating the public from the private man within his book, Howells in a sense violated the implication of its title, for his Mark Twain turned out to be a person not a *persona*, the man behind the mask an often difficult chap. Yet the public had their Mark Twain, and they have him yet, a Mark Twain who has not changed much since 1901, when Thomas Bailey Aldrich wrote to Howells that "Mark's spectacular personality is just now very busy all over the world. I doubt if there is another man on earth whose name is more familiar."

But Aldrich hung a mighty reservation from "just now," for he seems to have felt that it would be with Mark Twain as it had been with Robert Louis Stevenson, whose "surviving friends, still under the glamor of what must have been a winning personality, are hurting him by overpraise, and will end by getting him generally disliked." Aldrich had a theory, he told Howells, "that every author while living has a projection of himself, a sort of eidolon that goes about in near and distant places and makes friends and enemies for him out of folk who never know him in the flesh. When the author dies this phantom fades away, not caring to continue business at the old stand. Then the dead writer lives only in the impression made by his literature." Aldrich seems to imply that he (and Howells) had something less in the way of eidolons than their mutual friend, but that their works would outlast his, the Bad Boy surviving Tom Sawyer, Silas Lapham leaving Huck Finn behind. Aldrich was wrong, for like Walt Whitman, who had given the Greek word εἰδoλον current coinage, Mark Twain projected an image that—thanks to the camera—continues to prevail, remaining inseparable from the works that still bring him fame.

Nine years after Aldrich wrote his letter to Howells, and at the same time as Howells published his memoir-as-memorial, there appeared Professor Archibald Henderson's *Mark Twain,* a book that bore the prophetic motto *Désormais* ("henceforth"). Where William Dean Howells apparently heeded Aldrich's warning and rendered a fair-minded but hardly fair-headed portrait of Mark Twain, Henderson quoted Aldrich's letter as an epigraph to his book and then went on to laudatory lengths, as if to prove Aldrich wrong. He stressed Mark Twain's virtues not only as a man, but as "Humorist," "World-Famed Genius," and "Philosopher, Moralist, Sociologist," using terms generally reserved for Shakespeare and Goethe. Henderson was a professor of mathematics, not literature, and thereby enjoyed an amateur status that freed him from academic restraints. As a biographer and disciple of George Bernard Shaw, he seems to have delighted in shocking literary establishmentarians, for whom Mark Twain, as Henderson noted, was a mere humorist, only once removed from the "newspaper jokers."

Yet Henderson's adulation is couched in terms of familiarity, a note that

To operate, flip the next thirty-four pages between thumb and forefinger.

holds from the first sentence of his preface: "There are today, all over the world," he wrote, "men and women and children who owe a debt of almost personal gratitude to Mark Twain for the joy of his humor and the charm of his personality." This was the eidolon connection, and in discharging his own indebtedness by reaching for hyperbole in his discussion of Mark Twain's writings, Henderson continued to evoke a highly personal image. Though his own acquaintance with Clemens was slight, Henderson, unlike Howells, preferred the familiar "Mark," and thereby set the style for later writers—including professors—who never even met the man. Samuel Langhorne Clemens may have been lying in his grave, but his eidolon was marching on: "Mark Twain was one of the supreme literary geniuses of his time," Henderson asserted, "but he was something even more than this. He was not simply a great genius: he was a great man." Critics since have differed with Henderson's literary judgments and have mitigated somewhat his enthusiasm for Mark Twain as a "great [i.e., good] American," but they have never been able to detach the man himself from the books he wrote.

It was particularly appropriate therefore that Henderson accompany his text with photographic portraits of Mark Twain by Alvin Langdon Coburn, an associate of Stieglitz and Steichen and a friend of G. B. Shaw. And the eidolon preserved by Coburn is the Mark Twain we all know and love so well, the wise old man in white—whether his suit or bedsheets. When propped up by pillows, Henderson's sage in Coburn's picture not a little resembles one of those formaldehydrated saints of the communist world, on permanent display in his tomb. In 1911 such lavish illustration was relatively rare in literary biopsies,

but not subsequently, at least where Mark Twain is concerned. In this, as in so much, Archibald Henderson established the mode for subsequent scholar-critics. And it may be said that in so doing he also gave perpetuity to the

19

eidolon of Mark Twain as a literary patriarch, an image acceptable to the genteel tradition that had enshrined the Fireside Poets. But there was another, earlier Mark Twain, a jokester in part responsible for the fact that the number of eminent men of letters who had acknowledged his literary greatness could be counted (in 1910) on the fingers of one foot.

Even William Dean Howells did not fall into friendship with Mark Twain at first sight, being chagrined by his profane "breadth of parlance" and his Western flair for wearing fur coats "with the fur out," and Howells had frequent occasion to be embarrassed both by and for his friend ever afterward. Like his earliest writings, Mark Twain's eidolon was at first gauged to reach the hearts and minds (or "belly and bowels," as he put it) of the broadest but not the most refined segment of American society, the mass of the "people" with whom he was defiantly to identify himself in public while living in private the life few Rileys (even James Whitcomb) could afford. But under the influence of the Eastern environment, which included his wife, Olivia Langdon, and William Dean Howells, Mark Twain mended his manners, both literary and personal. As Henderson saw it, "the civilization of the East, its culture and refinement, tempered the genius of Mark Twain in conformity with the indispensable criteria of classic art."

One result was *The Prince and the Pauper,* in Henderson's eyes a result of the East's "persistent nationalism," which imbued Mark Twain "with the comprehensive ideals of American democracy," much as *Joan of Arc* bears the impress of the South, being "a pure work of the heart, the chivalric impulse of a noble spirit." The West, however, continued to prevail in the "virginal spontaneity of his native style . . . the vigor of his thought . . . the primitiveness of his expression," and his sartorial tastes tended to follow suit. "He was always," Howells recalled, "rather aggressively indifferent about dress," wearing a perpetual "suit of black serge, truly deplorable in the cut of the sagging frock." And yet, as the century turned so did Mark Twain's sense of himself, the writer going public in a number of ways, becoming a barking dog at the heels of imperialism—whether at home or abroad. Along with this change of voice came a different costume, Mark Twain shedding his modest black serge suit for one that symbolized his crusade on behalf of the oppressed, including a cape.

All that was wrong in America and the world was epitomized for Mark Twain by Theodore Roosevelt, whose Big-Stick-and-Soft-Voice diplomacy seemed equivalent to the apostolic Serpent-and-Dove of the missionary formula. Though few of his "bitter and caustic words upon a certain strenuous, limelight American politician" (as Archibald Henderson tactfully phrased it) ever saw print during his lifetime, Mark Twain most certainly gave the missionaries hell. As Anti-Christian, Mark Twain donned a wolf-in-lamb's-wool uniform, but his suit of gleaming white serge had other meanings as well. To New Englanders it suggested the vestiture of sainthood, while Southerners would recognize it as aristocratic (planters') garb, and Westerners thought it sufficiently outrageous to please. In effect, Clemens became Superb Sam, counterpart to our star-spangled Uncle, and very much the beloved cynosure of the public eye. The imperialists had the Great White Fleet, but the others had Mark Twain.

He had earned the right to white in other ways besides writing his fiery gospels. By 1907, when Mark Twain first put on his famous outfit, he had as the saying goes paid his dues by getting out of debt, redeeming himself of the cardinal American sin, bankruptcy. Having lost in his sixtieth year a fortune through unwise, even maniacal, investments—chief of which was that marvelous machine, Paige's mechanical typesetter—and having recovered his losses by going out once again on the lecture circuit, which he by then loathed, Mark Twain had atoned for whatever authorial and sartorial offenses he had earlier committed. Moreover, in paying off his creditors dollar for dollar owed, Mark Twain preserved his honor and recalled to the minds of the literati that earlier saint of Victorian letters, Sir Walter Scott (whom he detested). In Henderson's words, "the beautiful spirit of this great soul shone brightest in disaster."

Mark Twain in his first rise from a newsman's rags to a writer's riches had undergone that rite of passage intrinsic to the Protestant Epic, joining the ranks of such American heroes as Horatio Alger and Thomas Alva Edison. But in losing his first million and then regaining it, Mark Twain was twice purified, and was elevated thenceforth into the highest circle of thrones and denominations—where plaster icons become the purest marble—paired in many eyes with Abraham Lincoln. Father Abraham earned his halo by being martyred, while Mark Twain took the slower road; but by the turn of the century he was entitled to appear white-headed and transfigured in the beauty of the iris on the cover of *American Authors* (*Men*) as gatekeeper to the gallery of immortals-in-waiting. Nor would some of them, as E. F. Harkins nervously reminded his readers, have long to wait.

23

CHAPTER 3

Old age like death row is a powerful eradicator of sins, and Mark Twain by 1900 was becoming something of a memento mori in the literary world, forever associated with the exaggerated report of his death. He had already lost his favorite daughter, Susy, whom he publicly enshrined in *Joan of Arc,* and in 1904 his wife, Livy, died, to be followed by another daughter, Jean, in 1909. By the time Mark Twain joined this funereal procession, he was survived by only one child, Clara, who stubbornly resisted the family fate, and if it may be said that the whole world mourned her father's death, it must be added that Clara's sighs were probably those of relief. As the Man in White, Mark Twain was something of an unholy ghost where Clara was concerned, for his perturbed spirit was apt as he grew older to manifest itself in disconcerting and often public ways—including the wearing of white in prominent places. Clara, moreover, was ambitious to succeed as a concert singer and resented the persistence of her father's fame, whereas he in turn seems to have been jealous of her ambition, nor did he much approve of the young men whose company she kept.

Something of the complexity of their relationship is suggested by the fact that Clara left off singing soon after her father died and devoted the next half-century to keeping Mark Twain's eidolon in good repair. Though twice married, Clara Clemens Gabrilowitsch Samossoud remained wedded lifelong to Mark Twain, and she made sure that nothing from his dead hand would cause her the embarrassment the man himself had brought her when alive. In exorcising that mischievous ghost, Clara by necessity gave greater stature to the saint, and it was largely the result of her labors that Mark Twain was celebrated as being not only larger but better than life during the years after his death. Mo-

25

tivated by a combination of prudery and prudence, Clara as vestigial virgin became keeper of the fame she had earlier resented.

A writer for money, Mark Twain had been careful, even in his attacks on political bodies, not to offend any considerable proportion of the body politic—for no man is more democratic than he who is about to run for or open an office. And Clara, as beneficiary of his copyrights, renewed them regularly and, as steward of the keys to Mark Twain's unpublished papers, kept careful watch over the contents of what was put into posthumous print. For her, Mark Twain was like George Washington, a funding father intimately associated with the dollar bill, and Clara became a veritable Parson Weems where the going myth was concerned. Holding back Mark Twain's blasphemous *Letters from the Earth* until she herself was under ground, Clara did what she could also to keep Sam Clemens' most unattractive qualities buried, standing guard over a family vault stuffed full of family skeletons. Most of them grin out of the latter sections of Mark Twain's *Autobiography*, that haunted house where his ghost still walks, shrieking curses against the damned human race—not in general terms but in the most grisly particulars.

In 1901 E. F. Harkins quoted Mark Twain concerning the autobiography, a book he described as one not to be opened "until he has been in the grave for a century." But Harkins opined with a tolerant style that "so far as the main facts are concerned . . . the humorist's autobiography is already an open book. It has been chronicled piece by piece in a hundred magazines and in a thousand newspapers. . . . Probably no other living author has been so beset by the requests of editors and the importunities of reporters; and assuredly no other living author has been more amiable or more liberal in his responses. . . . Mark Twain's career has been public property, with no signs, no fences, not even a dog therein to bark at night." Mark Twain's autobiography, Harkins predicted, with one of his characteristic mortuary nudges, "will be submitted to the public within a hundred hours after his death." He was referring of course to the obituary that already lay on ice in newspaper morgues all over the country, but as a matter of fact Mark Twain began to publish sections of his *Autobiography* before he died, part of a complex scheme to renew his copyrights—for if his career was open daily to the public, his literary property was not. True, what sections Mark Twain allowed to be published bore out the lovable old image enshrined on the cover of *American Authors (Male)*, but had its editor had the opportunity to hearken to the Mark Twain who spoke from beyond the grave, he would have considerably altered his opinion. An autobiography in the tradition of neither Augustine nor Rousseau, Mark Twain's true confessions are in the American grain, which in his particular case has the distinction of being doubly crossed.

The model for American autobiography was written by Ben Franklin and was integral to his greatest invention, himself, being an exercise in self-canonization. But even the original Clean Old Man could not keep his benign smile from lifting in a slight sneer from time to time, for Franklin used his life story to dump a little dirt on the graves of defeated competitors, stupid business partners, and an occasional poet. And when Mark Twain's turn came to stand before the magic mirror of self-glorification, he indulged in whole chapters of vituperation, portraying himself not as the victor over but as the victim of his business associates, the men whom he depended upon to make him a Hartford Croesus but who instead (as he saw it) led him down the gilt-edged path to bankruptcy. "It was not ingratitude that he ever minded," wrote Howells; "it was treachery that really maddened him past forgiveness."

But Howells neglected to note that treachery was for Clemens what lechery was for other men, a matter of lust given velocity by an active imagination. And nothing was more certain to bring black bile pouring out of the white old man than business dealings, at which he was a hopelessly infatuated amateur whose mistakes were always to the disastrous disadvantage (and eternal damnation) of others. For Mark Twain was a very acrobat at turning the blame for his losses on those around him. In public he was willing to laugh at himself but in private he was not, and whether the game was billiards or business, he was a very sore loser. When he could fire the men he thought had betrayed him he would, and when he could not fire he would sue, and when he couldn't sue (or while he was waiting for the wheels of justice to turn) he would write libelous letters-to-the-editor concerning the real and (mostly) imaginary sins against him.

Much of this, being unprintable, ended up in his *Autobiography*, which with added touches of hellfire became a subterranean hall of defamation, the author being the man in charge of his private Inferno. The result is an epic of ill-sorts, and since the effect of the epical mode is to elevate, the *Autobiography*, like Pope's *Dunciad*, works against its satiric intention. Where Ben Franklin's adversaries are dismissed summarily, becoming incidental bugs caught in the amber of his jaundiced style, Mark Twain actually magnifies his enemies, until they become fit antagonists for his melodramatic stage. Ben is master of his rivals while Mark Twain makes himself over into the classic victim of greed, the Overreacher, a fool of his own creation. He ends up a terrifying burlesque upon that characteristic hero of the Gilded Age, the Business Man, a perverse flowering of the bulbous Franklin's Self-Made image.

Mark Twain in his *Autobiography* collapses at the last into fear and loathing, writing unmailed poison-pen letters which suggest that his humor shares more than an initial aspirant with hate. Though redeemed in the eyes of the public after his financial fall, Mark Twain remained within a private hell, from whence he saw God as the great trickster and himself as the ultimate victim—hence his penultimate identification with the Devil. Especial targets of his envious wrath were Bret Harte and Andrew Carnegie, the one for his failures (including unpaid debts to S.L.C.), the other for his success. They inspired tirades that border on the pathological, like the obsessive rage with which a man goes about pursuing a mosquito that has interrupted his sleep. Still, Mark Twain sufficiently retained his sanity to recognize that his attacks on associates and friends were the kinds of "truths" that must be spoken from the grave, the only place where such liberties cannot be taken into court as libelous.

Clara Clemens shared this wisdom and knew also that Mark Twain's apoplectic fits profited her little where his eidolon was concerned. Though much of the *Autobiography*—the earlier, funny, and nostalgic parts—saw print in 1924, Clara did not allow the most volcanic stuff to surface until 1940, as *Mark Twain in Eruption,* by which time his victims (and many copyrights) had expired. In her efforts to keep her father's darker side hidden, Clara was aided by the head priest in the temple to which she kept the keys, Mark Twain's literary executor, Albert Bigelow Paine, who edited the *Autobiography* and revised the devil out of *The Mysterious Stranger*. Paine also wrote the "official" life of Mark Twain, dedicated without intentional irony to the woman "who steadily upheld the author's purpose to write history rather than eulogy as the story of her father's life." But as history Paine's book is a massive demonstration of revisionist hagiography, relying heavily on Mark Twain's own carefully filtered recollections of his boyhood and youth and screened further through Clara's immaculate sieve.

Paine was Mark Twain's Boswell, a constant companion in his old age, always good for a game of billiards or cards and a master of appreciative laughter—even when he was the butt of the joke. Paine's only desire, he said, was "to serve him," for "it was a privilege and an honor to give him happiness," and if the language and attitude are those of a loyal servant, that is because as biographer Paine was something of a valet, adjusting his master's costume for best effect but never letting us into the secrets of the bedchamber. Like many servants, moreover, Paine, in taking care of Mark Twain, took care to serve himself as well, for by keeping the eidolon polished, he purveyed an image that would prove most attractive to the largest number of buyers. Though hardly as uncritical an adulator as Henderson, and avoiding the cozy "Mark" for the objective "Clemens," Paine nonetheless considerably tempered Howells's saving reservations with a holier-than-I prose style. While not neglecting Mark Twain's faults, Paine treated them in such a way that around each of the great man's warts there appears a tiny halo:

Mark Twain understood the needs of men because he was himself supremely human. . . . With his strength he had inherited the weaknesses of our kind. With him, as with another, a myriad of dreams and schemes and purposes daily flitted by. With him, as with another, the spirit of desire led him often to a high mountain-top, and was not rudely put aside, but lingeringly—and often invited to return. With him, as with another, a crowd of jealousies and resentments, and wishes for the ill of others, daily went seething and scorching along the highways of the soul. With him, as with another, regret, remorse, and shame stood at the bedside during long watches of the night; and in the end, with him, the better thing triumphed—forgiveness and generosity and justice—in a word, Humanity.

In two words, Jesus Christ! who for Mark Twain was more expletive than redeemer, and who had a middle initial H—for Hellfire not Humanity. For Mark Twain, at least in his last years, was more of Satan's party than of the Savior's, and when he went with the Tempter to the mountaintop, it was a race to see who got there first.

According to Archibald Henderson, Mark Twain was an "embodiment of the national spirit," an "incarnation of democratic America," but by 1912 A. B. Paine had elevated him to apotheotic heights, not so much by expunging the personal failings of which Henderson was ignorant as by reducing them to glorious generalities. Yet his portrait of Mark Twain is the fullest as well as the most fulsome we have, and his Mark Twain will probably remain the accepted version, if only because it is Hal Holbrook's too. Paine's mortuary and monumental prose is fleshed out in the manner of Henderson's book, with photo-

graphs of his subject taken by Paine himself—who spent a period of his youth as a professional photographer—camera work which, like his biographical point of view, evinces tricks of composition and light that show his subject to advantage. Many of the best-known pictures of Mark Twain as white old man were taken by him, some of which appeared in the first edition of the biography and in the several volumes of the author's work that Paine edited under Clara's supervision. Though hardly a camera artist comparable to Coburn, Paine had considerable talent, and his efforts contributed mightily to the persistence of Mark Twain's saintly eidolon, which continued long after the death of Samuel L. Clemens to help convert his copyrights into cash.

Mark Twain and his biographer playing parallel pool.

Camera Obscura

Because of his photographer's eye, Paine in his biography tends to lapse into language informed by camera work, seeing Mark Twain as through a view finder. The result is a perfect marriage of subject and style, as in his description of an early encounter by the biographer with Mark Twain:

I ought to state that he was in bed when we arrived, and that he remained there during almost all of these earlier dictations [of his *Autobiography,* which Paine relied on heavily for his account of Clemens' early years], clad in a handsome silk dressing-gown of rich Persian pattern, propped against great snowy pillows. He loved this loose luxury and ease, and found it conducive to thought. On the little table beside him, where lay his cigars, papers, pipes, and various knickknacks, shone a reading lamp, making more brilliant the rich coloring of his complexion and the gleam of his shining hair. There was daylight, too, but it was north light, and the winter days were dull. Also the walls of his room were a deep, unreflecting red, and his eyes were getting old. The outlines of that vast bed blending into the luxuriant background, the whole focusing to the striking central figure, remain in my mind today—a picture of classic value.

As picture, it resembles the painterly ensemble by Coburn which decorates as frontispiece Henderson's book, and Paine himself soon took advantage of his intimate situation to capture the image on film. Among the pictures that resulted was "one in an attitude which had grown so familiar to us, that of leaning over to get his pipe from the smoking-table, and this seemed to give him particular satisfaction," with the result that the attitude has become familiar to the rest of the world.

35

As in the description of Mark Twain in bed, the dictation of the *Autobiography* supplied Paine with several memorable moments, especially during the first year of their association. When Mark Twain was not dictating from his bed, he would do so pacing up and down, and especially dramatic were the pacings at Upton House, a summer place in New Hampshire that Mark Twain rented in 1906, where a long veranda provided a deck upon which the old man would pace "up and down before that panoramic background. . . . When I think of that time I shall always hear the ceaseless, slippered, shuffling walk, and see the white figure with its rocking, rolling movement passing up and down the long gallery, with that preternaturally beautiful landscape behind." To insure this recollection, Paine seems to have taken a picture of that too, and so strong was the association of the *Autobiography* and Paine's picture taking that Mark Twain included a sequence of shots in the book itself, giving the paragraphs unity by means of a mischievous little monologue,

"Shall I Be Good?"

No. 1

Shall

I learn to
be good? . . . . .
. . . .
I will sit
here and
think it
over.

Truly Yours

Mark Twain

Sept.
'06.

No. 2

More do seem
to be so many
diffi . . . . .

☞

37

But these pictures did not appear in the version of the *Autobiography* edited by Paine; instead, when gathered together in the great Stormfield Edition of Mark Twain's works in 1929, the preponderance of photographs taken by his biographer leaves no question where goodness is concerned, being uniformly sedate and saintly shots.

.... and there's so many other privileges, that .... perhaps .....

0.6.

7

Oh, never mind, reckon I'm good enough just as I am.

39

Whether
posed like a waxwork with books and calabash pipe,

or fixed in a single frame in his rocking chair,

the effect is entirely static and one-dimensional, a pasteboard figure propped up like an advertisement under the marquee of a theater. Along with Tom Sawyer's fence it is a whitewash job starring the old filmflam man himself, and in this sense at least Paine's biography is true to the man whose name appears on the

41

cover, not Samuel L. Clemens but Mark Twain, an eidolon not only laundered but starched and pressed flat.

As cardboard cutup, Mark Twain was all ready for the ordeal to which his eidolon was subjected by Van Wyck Brooks in 1920, for if he went into his grave a saint he was hauled out and desecrated ten years later for a holy sinner, less a product of triumphant democracy than an artifact of American manufacture. For Brooks portrayed Mark Twain as a natural-born writer who was warped by the commercial spirit of his age, a "starved artist who for forty years . . . had to pretend that he was a business man . . . the saddest, the most ironical figure in all the history of this Western continent," a cross between a comet and a sewing-machine salesman. No pictures accompanied Brooks's text—a significant omission—and whatever its effect upon the literati, the book seems to have had little impact upon the reading public. Under the supervision of Paine, Mark Twain's saintly eidolon continued to glow in the marketplace and in the homeplace too, until such a time as Fredric March could make the young and Holbrook the old man flesh.

Justin Kaplan it was who, in *Mr. Clemens and Mark Twain* (1966), gave widespread circulation to the image as rearranged by Brooks, less as "the supreme victim of an epoch in American history" than as a casualty of his own epical greed. If Mark Twain as Western Genius was a prostitute to Moloch, it was because like many another cowboy he put himself on the Street. Even in his acts of redemption, his attacks on imperialistic adventurers, he remained silent concerning his several capitalist friends, especially the Standard Oil magnate Henry Huttleston Rogers, who was instrumental in helping him recover his wealth.

Torn by these and other conflicts, the man who stares out of the final pages of Kaplan's book appears to be ravaged with the pangs of guilt (or, as in the famous portrait of Dr. Johnson, the pains of gas, for Sam the incarnate American like Sam the epitomized Briton suffered from both). Photographs like this are the kinds of evidence Clara Clemens kept from sight, pictorial counterpart to Mark Twain's last, embittered railings against God, but it—and the writings—are only part of a complex whole. The division of his personality was hardly so simple as the dichotomy outlined by Kaplan, for the man contained more pairs than a chess set or a shoe store. Still, Kaplan's Twain made it impossible any longer to view Mr. Clemens through the lens of Albert Paine's camera, but rather, as with a stereoscope, rendered an image much closer to life. To better comprehend the vengeful ghost, we need both Hyperion and the satyr.

For all his cosmic cosmetics, Albert Bigelow Paine had hold of a central truth about Mark Twain: not only was the man behind the mask greatly—even grossly—human, but his was a transcendent presence for all (perhaps even because) of that, a compound of marvels approximating art. And as art it was theater. "Mark Twain's appearance on the stage of the world," writes Paine, "was a succession of dramatic moments. He was always exactly in the setting. Whatever he did or whatever came to him, was timed for the instant of greatest effect. At the end he was more widely observed and loved and honored than ever before, and at the right moment and in the right manner he died." Mark Twain in his old age was a fatalist, for whom the driving force of event was circumstance—"kismet"—and looking back in his *Autobiography*, he saw his own life as a dramatic series of turning points. Paine shares the perspective—and ac-

cepted the author's occasional revisions of fact—and despite our reservations regarding Paine's objectivity, we may also view the major phases of Mark Twain's life as assuming the patterns of drama. Starting with the apparently circuitous path of his early years, the Mississippi youth and Western young manhood, by the end of the second act the plot line has assumed straight lines, the steady upward climb toward prosperity and fame, with its Eastern setting. Then in the fourth act come reverses, a descent that Mark Twain's recovery of his wealth did not much affect, and in the fifth act comes the tragedy that Paine depicted in terms of transcendence.

The proximity of Mark Twain's life to art is a contingency strengthened by the fact that his most famous writings were abstracted from his personal past. Similarly, in his travel books Mark Twain gave form to events by witnessing, even at times (in the best tradition of modern journalism) creating, them, much as the landscape is clarified by the passage of the sun—or a tramp. In all his writings fiction mingles with fact to a greater or lesser degree, much as the line between Mark Twain and Samuel L. Clemens is finally indistinguishable, the mask having fused to the face. Thus as his fiction is heavily autobiographical, so his *Autobiography* is at times pure invention, and his inventions are the stuff that dreams are made of. Paine merely gave this conjunction life after death by extending it through his biography, and in concealing certain salient aspects of Mark Twain's last years, he gave added validity to the popular image of the beloved old man—a Prospero who makes his peace with the world before leaving it. In truth, however, when the time came to make his final exit, Mark Twain was closer to Lear.

45

CHAPTER 5

Mark from the Tomb

In 1866 Mark Twain advertised his first public lecture by announcing that "the trouble begins at eight," and regarding his final private performance it might be said that the disaster commenced at seventy. Hamlin Hill has recently chronicled the last decade of Mark Twain's life: in *Mark Twain: God's Fool* he projects something less than E. F. Harkins' saintly image, showing instead how the pessimism and fragmentariness of Mark Twain's last writings reflect the lost purpose and blurred focus that was his life after Livy's death. Surrounded by well-meaning attendants like Paine, who fondly and worshipfully called him "King," Clemens, like one of Shakespeare's tragic monarchs (or Howard Hughes), was kept insulated from the importuning world but could not, finally, be protected from himself.

He was seldom alone but seems always to have been lonely, and his daughters were almost never at home. Clara was off pursuing her career and Jean, a victim of epilepsy, was hounded by madness through a succession of asylums, and when she finally returned to live with her father, it was only to die suddenly, providing the material for the last entry in Mark Twain's *Autobiography*. A year later Clemens himself was dead, the most famous family man in America reunited with his wife and most of their children. Though his death was attributed to that mysterious disease of the heart, angina, like the word itself it may be said to have stemmed from a deep-rooted anger, which as grief slowly throttled him in its torturing, vinelike grip. "It's down in de bills dat you's gwyne to git hung" is the fate prophesied for Huck by Jim, and though we do not know how Huck finally died, strangulation is a death that dogged the twin tragic geniuses of nineteenth-century fiction, Ahab and Mark Twain, the two of them snared at the last by a cosmic whiteness of their own creation, equivalent to the nothingness that overwhelms King Lear.

In effect, by hiding these facts, Albert Bigelow Paine played Nahum Tate whereas Hamlin Hill has restored the darker parts of the drama's last act. In so doing he lends Mark Twain's final years the tragic shape that the writer in his works was never able to attain, giving his death a "rightness" we associate with the highest level of dramatic art. But in correcting Paine's facts, Hill, if anything, makes Paine's dramatic analogy all the more valid, suggesting that the biographer wrote more truly than he let on. And Paine was certainly accurate when he spoke of the universally loved and honored old man who was viewed on his bier by grieving thousands. Whatever else he was beneath his mask, as a public person Mark Twain was a polished performer with a nearly faultless platform sense, and though his old age may be seen in dramatic terms as a tragedy, as a creature of the theater Mark Twain was a King who kept his Fool up stage until the last scene. Even in his final illness he stayed a funny man, writing Paine from Bermuda that he was unwilling to die there, "for this is an unkind place for a person in that condition. I should have to lie in the undertaker's cellar until the ship would remove me & it is dark down there & unpleasant."

Yorick's skull is more than a memento mori, and humor transcends its bones. Like time it is a valuable commodity that depends upon complex works and a certain tension at the core, but we destroy it by attempting to remove the hands and face. The mechanisms of Mark Twain's psyche, like the parts of a clock, contain a fascination of their own, quite apart from their public function, but it is a mistake to separate the two. As with Pope's creatures and Words-

47

worth's beauteous things we murder to dissect, ending up with a handful of tics but not much more. And if it may be said that Sam Clemens, like Grandfather's Clock, never knew when to quit, then it must be added that Mark Twain had a marvelous sense of timing. As a consummate actor he was finally consumed by his role—like the greatest entertainers a cipher finally, a zero at the bones—but in the end he obeyed the comedian's highest law and left them laughing.

Peering down at the remains of his dead friend Mark Twain, William Dean Howells reflected on the essential duality of the man when alive, the comedian as cynical savant, the tragedian as clown: "I looked a moment at the face I knew so well; and it was patient with the patience I had so often seen in it: something of a puzzle, a great silent dignity, an assent to what must be from the depths of a nature whose tragical seriousness broke in the laughter which the unwise took for the whole of him." Howells was the one who called Mark Twain the "Lincoln of our Literature," an epithet joining in holy patrimony the two great Westerners of the age, in whom were conjoined elements of comedy and tragedy, an uneasy union that once again evokes the Shakespearean mode. Yet differences remain, for as the public Lincoln endures in a tragic guise, Mark Twain retains his comic pose, forever a man of the popular stage, ready whenever the curtains open to go on. Lincoln broods in the shadows of his Memorial, a tragic titan surrounded by his noble words, while Mark Twain lives on in his *Autobiography*, from whence may be heard the jingling of a jester's bells, fit accompaniment to the mad ravings of a tormented king.

Mark Twain the entertainer was a master of one-liners, wry epigrams better suited for almanacs and calendars than for the entablatures of public buildings—being memorable unto the day thereof but not much beyond. Archibald Henderson testifies that Mark Twain's wit and wisdom crackled through the air in 1910 like the earliest messages sent by Marconi, but for the most part his saws and sayings have been forgotten. Even his best-known pronouncement, "Everybody talks about the weather, but nobody does anything about it," was actually the work of his friend and literary collaborator, Charles Dudley Warner, a bona fide Connecticut Yankee who also gave us "Politics makes strange bedfellows" but not much else. Yet Mark Twain *was* a funny man, an extremely funny man, whose humor can still make us laugh. That is why we forgive him his sins, for his was a valuable talent if grotesque, like the toad, without which no garden is complete.

Still, Mark Twain resurrected for an evening is a masterpiece of selective editing, a slim ghost of the long row of works that lies a-moldering on the shelf. Much of what he wrote is eminently forgettable, being of the essence ephemeral, and of a piece with the life which was its material and its occasion, both highly impromptu in character and circumstantial in causation. The famous period piloting steamboats on the great river was chiefly valuable to Mark Twain the writer as a vanished way of life, and the frontier that he recorded in *Roughing It* was melting away like the silver ores of Nevada even as he departed for the East. He commenced his creative career as a writer for that most frangible of mediums, the newspaper, and it was as a comic lecturer that he first became famous, giving performances whose hilarity depended in large

CHAPTER 6

Papier Macher

Wit and Humor

OF THE AGE

COMPRISING

Wit, Humor, Pathos, Ridicule,

SATIRES, DIALECTS, PUNS.

Conundrums, Riddles, Charades,

JOKES AND MAGIC.

BY

MARK TWAIN,	ROBT. J. BURDETTE,
JOSH BILLINGS,	ALEX. SWEET,
	ELI PERKINS.

WITH

THE PHILOSOPHY OF WIT AND HUMOR.

BY

MELVILLE D. LANDON, A.M.

Illustrated

CHICAGO.
STAR PUBLISHING CO.,
1894.

part on the magical presence of the actor, an electrical and evanescent component that, when gone, leaves things even flatter than before.

Forty years after he began "playing professional humorist before the public," Mark Twain recollected in his *Autobiography* that he had been but one of "seventy-eight other American humorists," each of whom "rose in my time, became conspicuous and popular, and by and by vanished." Of these many "sparkling transients" only Mark Twain endured, and he prevailed, he thought, because he was not a "mere" humorist, but was something of a teacher and a preacher as well. Still, even sermons have a certain term, which he defined as thirty years (two more than the copyright law then protected), for "the very things humor preaches about and which are novelties when it preaches about them can cease to be novelties and become commonplaces in thirty years." Though perhaps an exercise in false modesty, Mark Twain's prediction was on the whole quite accurate, for the books and stories that still secure his fame represent only a fraction of his published works. It is once again the matter and the man, and if the man gave the matter the gift of life, it did not live long after he died. As material it was like his medium ephemeral, much as his image comes down to us not in monumental stone but as pictures printed on handbills, posters, photographs, advertisements, and as illustrations in books.

Mark Twain rose to fame and fortune on a tide of cheap paper, pulp turned out by a sulfur process and high-speed rotary presses, and if the last guaranteed wide circulation of his works, the first insured they would not long endure as objects, dooming his books to certain oblivion. Like the picture of Mark Twain in flames excised at his wife's command from *Life on the Mississippi,* the writer's

corpus is burning even as this is being written, its yellowing paper oxidizing slowly but inevitably until nothing remains but dusty ashes. This holds true for most books published during the last part of the nineteenth, and for much of the present, century, and Mark Twain is joined in flames (as he undoubtedly anticipated) by the same crowd that keeps him company in *Famous Authors (Men)*—nor are *Famous Authors (Women)* exempt from that common doom. But the fate seems particularly fitting for Mark Twain, who as Kineman was also Ephemeral Man, and Trashman as well. Along with the library of neglectable books he wrote, Mark Twain was the inventor of a line of unsalable goods, including "Adjustable and Detachable Straps for Garments," a number of children's games, a railroad steam brake, and cures for chilblains and piles. His one successful invention was entirely appropriate, a self-pasting scrapbook and hence a repository for the flotsam of a jetsam culture. On his last triumphant tour to England and back, undertaken to receive his Oxford degree, Mark Twain kept a secretary busy clipping and pasting newspaper and magazine accounts of the event, collecting the cloud of trash that attended his canonization.

As Trashman he was an incurable gadgeteer, being one of the first Americans to own a telephone and the first writer to compose on a typewriter, and he never seems to have tired trying out new fountain pens. The money he made from writing cheap books he lost by investing in a typesetter whose chief function was a never-ending and expensive need for further improvements. This habit was maintained by the profits from the sale of junk produced by Mark Twain's publishing company, whose printing press was something of a compacter, turning out (in Justin Kaplan's words) "a mishmash of undistinguished books by or about famous people." True, the publications of his company were not much different from the staples of publishers today, but that is precisely the point: from *The Life of Pope Leo XIII* to the latest "greatest book of the age" is an apostolic succession of sorts, certifying the primacy of Mark Twain as a saint of the marketplace, a nickel eidolon.

When his publishing house failed and he became a bankrupt, Mark Twain discovered the other side of fame. While out on his lecture tour he had to keep revising his routines so as to stay one step ahead of reporters who eagerly plagiarized them as "news." By then the circle had come full round, and the old newspaperman had become good copy himself, his public persona a symbol of both notoriety and evanescence. As papery patriarch he was attended thenceforth in the manner of his personal comet, being trailed by a tail of reporters and photographers, a picturesque old party tailormade for the rotogravures just beginning to appear. "Always remember," he told Dorothy Quick, a young acquaintance of his last years, "in America there is nothing so important to a person in the public eye as the Press." He ended his career as a public man by writing letters to the editor, an epistolary genre that he brought to perfection but that, like his letters from the grave, is short-lived as literature, because concerned with contemporary affairs.

That Mark Twain during these last years put on his pure white suit is one of those coincidences that illuminate in all directions. For not only was it a sign of his sainthood but it dramatizes his role as Ephemeral Man, a pasteboard masque that is the essence of American popular culture, a mystery that Mark

Twain in his whiteness symbolizes, much as Moby Dick stands for an eternal but no less equivocal myth. It is the lightning bug and the lightning (to borrow Mark Twain's phrase) or the Matterhorn in Disneyland and the one in the Alps. As official costume Mark Twain's showy garb is antithetical to the white dress favored by his reclusive contemporary, Emily Dickinson, yet like bride and groom they stand together on the same cake, the poet perversely shy in her bedroom, the pundit glad to be photographed and interviewed in his nightgown. Mark Twain's drawling garrulity and Emily Dickinson's screaming silence are the stuff of which eidolons are made, those products of divinity factories in which the whole in both its largeness and smallness is summed up by a single image, sweeping the present that has become the past into an infinite future, "from the whole resulting, rising at last and floating, / A round, full-orb'd eidolon."

Moby Twain

Mark Twain's first public appearance in white out of season was the highlight of a visit to Washington, D.C., made in December 1906, for the ostensible purpose of lobbying on behalf of improved copyright laws. When he removed his dark overcoat in the dimness of the congressional-committee room, the effect was electric, like a bulb going on or a stripteaser's dress coming off. He looked, wrote the adoring Paine, like a knight "in white armor," but to Howells (who was also there) he resembled a goddamned fool. "What in the world," hissed Howells to Paine, "did he wear that white suit for?" But then Howells was a convert to Bostonianism and more proper than pious, so it took a while before he appreciated what he had seen. "Nothing could have been more dramatic," he later recalled in *My Mark Twain*, "than the gesture with which he flung off his long loose overcoat, and stood forth in white from his feet to the crown of his silvery head. It was a magnificent *coup*, and he dearly loved a *coup*." As *coup de théâtre*, moreover, it was also a *coup plein de grâce*, an announcement in effect of Mark Twain's divine election to highest office. Violating the dress code for the sake of a greater good, Mark Twain's choice of the dazzling suit was appropriate to the occasion and the man, since both were intimately associated with copyrights. But as symbolic costume it had a further, even prophetic, reach, for the Man in the White Suit would soon be vying with the Man in the White House as a spokesman for the American people.

In his last years Mark Twain virtually abandoned authorship, but in the process of putting on the white suit he became literature—at least the litterature of the daily news. This was the heyday of yellow journalism, and no one gathered more hey than he, who soon became the rival of Outcault's Kid for the public eye. Mark Twain became a veritable tabloid rajah, conspiring with reporters and cameramen, so radiant in the flashlights' glare, so trenchant in the warfare of words. When Mark Twain traveled to England to receive his Oxford degree, he met the young George Bernard Shaw, then only fifty, and there was a laying on of hands as well as flattery. For during the second half of his Methuselah-like life, Shaw increasingly usurped Mark Twain's public pose, and was always good for a sharp grumble about the failings of the damned human race, much as his beard, acerb scowl, and scratchy tweeds (with knickers) provided photogenic equivalents to Mark Twain's perpetual white.

We are so used to Mark Twain's final image we tend to forget that it represents but four of his forty years before the public, that there is another image equally familiar to his contemporaries, one lacking the saintly, long-suffering dimension. Though hardly an ugly man, Mark Twain at the start of his career had the face of a comedian, with reddish hair (considered like laughter to be vulgar by proper Victorians), small, shrewd blue eyes, a large nose (James Russell Lowell, an obsessive Jew-finder, thought it was Semitic), and a mustache that varied in length like a lawn. This Mark Twain was distressing to his family, provoking daughterly despair to which the articulate Susy gave voice: "They think of Mark Twain as a humorist joking at everything, 'And with a mop of reddish brown hair which sorely needs the barbars brush a roman nose, short stubby mustache, a sad careworn face, with maney crow's feet,' etc. That is the way people picture papa."

Instead, said Susy, "he has beautiful gray hair, not any too thick or any too long, but just right; a Roman nose, which greatly improves the beauty of

his features; kind blue eyes and a small mustache." The Roman nose remains a central feature of the image, but the landscape around is considerably manicured, a metamorphosis that dates, with the gray hair, from about 1885. It was at this same time also that "papa" began to wear suits of gray "to match his hair and eyes," even carrying on his shoulder a little gray kitten, "a mighty pretty sight! The gray cat sound asleep against papa's gray coat and hair." The gray effect suggests still one more motive for his latter-day saintly garb—uniformity of aesthetic effect—but this exterior redecoration seems also to reflect an attempt at protective coloration, especially since it dates from Mark Twain's first efforts to be accepted by the world of belles-lettres, as witnessed by his genteel and sentimental *The Prince and the Pauper*. Dedicated "To Those Good-Mannered and Agreeable Children, Susy and Clara Clemens," it pleased Mark Twain's daughters immensely. Susy thought it was "unquestionably the best book he has ever written . . . full of lovely charming ideas . . . that reveal something of his kind sympathetic nature." Like the good gray man, the pauper become prince, his story of royalty in rags has the mark of New England upon it, as Archibald Henderson noted.

Even as he combed his wild stylistic wool smooth, Mark Twain himself was shaved and shorn. Off came the sealskin coat whose fur had rubbed Howells the wrong way, on went genteel gray and somber black serge—as in this portrait by Barnett of London. Mark Twain came to detest a widely circulated photograph by Sarony which (he claimed) made him look like a gorilla in an overcoat, for the man who had once been a dandy in the Western mode became increasingly uncomfortable with reminders of his former self. As he grew

older, moreover, he became quite handsome and correspondingly vain, hence the final efflorescence. Still, the white suit was outrageous by any sartorial standard, and he gave it more panache by adding the matching cape, creating a flamboyant costume that not only flouted stylistic decorum but flaunted the wearer like a flag. It was, he told a nervous Clara and Jean, his "don'tcareadamn suit," being "a very beautiful costume" and both "stunning" and "conspicuous." His choice of words would not have reassured his doubtful daughters, but they tell us a great deal about Mark Twain's motive behind his mode, for if he didn't give a damn what people said, he most certainly (like P. T. Barnum) cared one hell of a lot that they said something.

Though he first put on his white suit in Washington, it was more truly a creation of New York City, where he lived on Fifth Avenue during the years following Livy's death. For if Hartford is Insurance City, a place where one plays it safe so as not to be sorry, New York is the Great White Way, and once again like a chameleon Mark Twain dressed to match. His companion-biographer Paine remarks frequently on "the fullness of his love for theatrical effect," which took (as Howells could have told him) a little getting used to. On their first Sunday walk in New York, Paine suggested they return home early "to avoid the throng," but Mark Twain informed him "quietly" that he *liked* the throng, and proceeded to form an Easter Parade of one, strolling up the Avenue into the pages of the rotogravures. "Of course," wrote Paine, "he was the object on which every passing eye turned; the presence to which every hat was lifted. I realized that this open and eagerly paid homage of the multitude was still dear to him . . . as the tribute of a nation, the expression of that affection

. . . he had declared to be the last and final and most precious reward that any man can win, whether by character or achievement. It was his final harvest, and he had the courage to claim it—the aftermath of all his years of honorable labor and noble living."

This again is the beloved parlor saint, described by one who knew him in his last years as a "charming, courteous gentleman, with a crown of silver hair [and] immaculate white clothes." But the same adoring pen spoke also of what was called "the S.L.C. Life-Saving Society," "a small circle of loving friends" who saw to it that the "guileless and unsuspecting" old man was never drawn by his "kind heart" "into annoying relationships . . . by designing and not altogether desirable strangers." Yet Mark Twain was perfectly capable of rescuing himself, having "a wonderful way of suddenly disappearing, of slipping into space, of melting into a misty background, when he wished to escape a person who bored him, that was the perfection of art." So the crowd-pleasing costume was also a kind of invisible cloak, the public saint being something of a private snob, and so far as the saintliness went, Mark Twain took care that his was not the perfect whiteness of plaster by shrouding himself with the satanic incense produced by tobacco. The result was both dramatic and oracular, "his white head and strong features enveloped in a cloud of smoke, out of which his voice came to us vibrating with . . . feeling," and it was also

a cartoonist's delight, as evidenced by the handiwork of A. S. Cox, which *The New York Times* saw fit to print.

Mark Twain's cigar was a personal signature equivalent to John Hancock's autograph and Charlie Chaplin's cane, being flamboyantly assertive and yet comic withal. It was, along with his outrageous suit, something of a prank, a fragrant violation of saintly shibboleths—including the homily against smoking in bed. Mark Twain's association with smoke is legendary and has meaning beyond the tobacco connection, being part of his infatuation with hellfire and damnation. As he lay on his deathbed, without power of speech, Mark Twain went through the motions of smoking a cigar, even exhaling an invisible cloud,

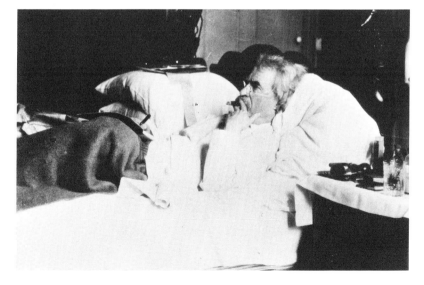

and then smiled, the great comedian a mime at the last, and still a man of smoke, a great white clown slowly fading away. His wraith of white hair helped to fill out the image that the greatest of caricaturists, Max Beerbohm, delineated, a pyromaniacal spirit that is also revealed in certain photographs, in which the satanic persona of his last stories and fragments pushes close to the skin.

Mark Twain worked for years on a story that was not published during his lifetime save in extracts, *Captain Stormfield's Visit to Heaven*, and in the last decade of his writing career he interminably revised, without finishing, *The Mysterious Stranger*. If the first bears out Huck Finn's contention that hell is a better place to spend eternity, the second suggests that purgatory is right here on this earth, literary evidence underwriting the somber dimension of Mark Twain's declining years. Much as he declared to Paine that he longed for death, having "had his tragedy," so his attendant cloud of smoke and halo of white hair provide a symbol of *carpe diem,* as in a cartoon by the British artist Nibs where he appears in a green suit and resembles a dandelion gone to seed. Mark Twain old is an emblem of mortality, a portrait of mutability impressed on paper or captured in the fading ghosts of silver nitrate negatives that melt away even as the paper of his books slowly decays. It is an image perfectly captured in one of A. L. Coburn's finest pictures, in which the man in white seems on the point of dissolving into mist and smoke, a romantic, idealized eidolon whose effect is mitigated only slightly by the knowledge that one of the reasons Mark Twain favored white was that he was pestered by a pernicious case of dandruff.

Houses of Mark

Mark Twain's theatricality, in terms of personal performance and the tendency of his life to assume the shape of drama—the stages remarked on by Paine—is borne out, even backed up, by the very houses that he lived in, commencing with the double cabin that his father, John Clemens, built in Florida, Missouri. Though Sam was actually born the year before it was built, for years this was celebrated as Mark Twain's birthplace, and eventually it was torn down to be broken up into souvenirs and sold. "No," Mark Twain said of this equivalent to the true cross, "it is too stylish, it is not my birthplace."

He also wrote, in his *Autobiography*, that "some one in Missouri has sent me a picture of the house I was born in. Heretofore I have always stated that it was a palace, but I shall be more guarded now." The inherent contradiction bears out Mark Twain's tendency to sacrifice consistency for momentary (and monetary) effect, but his emphasis on "style" and "palaces" is worth noting, given his later tastes in architecture. And the double cabin and Mark Twain's contradictory reactions to it have still another meaning, for both are symbolic of his inherent dichotomy, his psychic tendency to express himself in antithetical pairs, the twins that haunt his fiction from the start.

The most famous of Mark Twain's boyhood dwellings is the house in Hannibal, against which the world-famous author was photographed when he returned to his hometown in 1902. The picture of him posed in front of that humble clapboard house is one of the most recognizable icons from the American photographic record, a scrap from the Horatio Alger Album of Boys Who Made Good (and Plenty). But the lesser-known pictures recording the taking of the famous photograph are much more revealing, not only because they show the crowded scene behind the camera—the modern sign of celebrity status—but because they are reminiscent of the action on a motion-picture set, the panoply of apparatus necessary to create an often simple image. Thus the linearity of the final composition emphasizes the narrowness and restraints of village life abandoned by young Sam Clemens for the larger world, symbolized by the great river that groaned past Hannibal bearing its load of mud and merchandise. But the pictures *of* the picture tell another story, which has to do with the intimate relationship between the fame to which the river carried Mark Twain and its

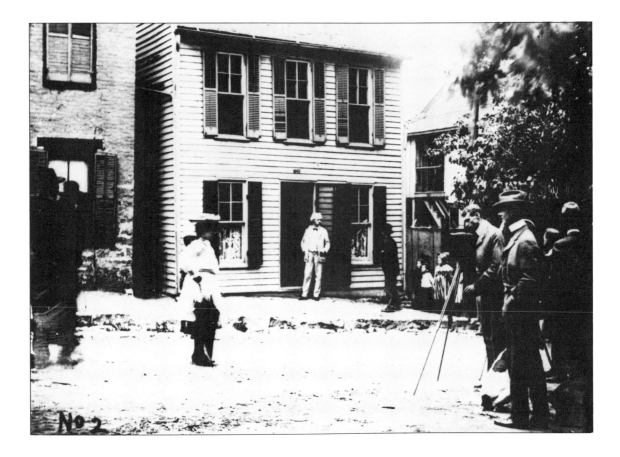

No 2

68

Mark Twain at his old home, Hannibal

cost in terms of privacy. The viewer of the finished picture feels alone with the great man, but he is only one in a vast crowd of admirers, each one pushing forward—as when the President passes by—motivated by a desire to kiss or kill. The net result is purely theatrical, a complex study in reality and illusion in which we can with difficulty (if at all) distinguish between the two.

Moving on and eastward, we come to the first house that Mark Twain owned—thanks to the generosity of his newly acquired father-in-law, Jarvis Langdon of Elmira, New York, a dealer in coal and security. The solid-looking brick house was located in Buffalo, where the bridegroom tried for a time to make his living as a newspaper editor-and-publisher, and as stage set it perfectly expresses the respectable middle-class life for which it stands. But Jarvis Langdon died shortly thereafter, and the Buffalo honeymoon did not much outlast his departure, for as soon as Mark Twain's writing began to pay off, he sold his paper and moved with his growing family to Hartford. Midway between the publishing capitals of Boston and New York, the capital city of Connecticut was a capital location for a professional writer, halfway between the literary influence of the one city and the business activity of the other. Suspended like Mahomet's coffin between the two was the famous brick Memorial, in which Mark Twain wrote his greatest books, was famous, raised his family, entertained the great, the near great, and Bret Harte. But it was there also that Mark Twain went broke pursuing the good life and even better fortune than the house represented. It was there also that Susy died, putting a close to a period and producing the tragic, white-haired old man, who never could bring himself to live in it thereafter. The only one of his several homes in whose

design Mark Twain had a hand, the Hartford Memorial belongs among his other works, and as cover the exterior does resemble the books that bear his name. Its steamboat gothicism has often been noted, but the likeness is a matter of incidental touches not main design, for as a structure the Hartford house, like so many of Mark Twain's works, has a rambling, eclectic, eccentric design, being an impromptu performance amounting to a frozen parade.

IRANISTAN.

The Hartford house was intended for a showplace, as theatrical within and without as any Hollywood set—or home—a demonstration in ostentatiousness, conspicuous consumption, and Tiffany-glass that is peculiarly American, reminding us that it was in nearby Bridgeport that P. T. Barnum erected Iranistan, a structure that (like its chief inhabitant) would be right at home in Disneyland. Though Barnum's elephantine barn burned down about the time young Sam Clemens was having his tintype taken, like a phoenix it would rise again in Hartford. In his autobiographical eruptions Mark Twain attacked Theodore Roosevelt for being "the Tom Sawyer of the political world," accusing him of "always showing off, always hunting for a chance to show off. In his frenzied imagination the Great Republic is a vast Barnum circus with him for a clown and the whole world for audience; he would go to Halifax for half a chance to show off, and he would go to hell for a whole one." As with so many of the persons crucified in Mark Twain's *Autobiography*, Roosevelt bears a certain resemblance to the author, who was after all (or so he maintained) the grand original of Tom Sawyer and who most certainly played the clown under the very big top of the Hartford house. As showplace, that is to say, it sheltered one of the greatest showoffs and showmen of all American time.

Like Barnum, Mark Twain was one of the first Americans to rise to wealth and prominence by entertaining the public with hoaxes and other fictions, and their houses likewise were marvels of fantasy and fun. But where Barnum's carlot Camelot was a glittering nineteenth-century equivalent of several miles of tinsel and neon tubes, being chiefly façade, Mark Twain's many-chambered mansion is at once a more human and a very complex structure. Its red brick exterior reflects the warmth of the man inside, yet the interior is a shadowy manifestation of his darker self. A lover of effect, even in architecture, Mark Twain had a window placed over his fireplace so he could watch the snow falling as he toasted his toes, yet another manifestation of his inner dualism, and the rest of the house followed suit, being like a good hand of cards full of tricks. Hallways and rooms are placed hither and yon, and the upper floors give way to Mark Twain's billiards-room retreat, the most important space in the house—and the one farthest away from the living room. By contrast, a Mississippi riverboat is a marvel in classic simplicity and straight lines, much closer in design to Barnum's house in that regard, its famous steamboat gothicism a matter chiefly of applied gingerbread. And if the pilot house was far removed from the passenger decks, the distance was more a manifestation of responsibility than escape, providing the quietude and visibility necessary to the pilot's task, a function that was only incidentally fun. What the pilot house did share with Mark Twain's billiards room was an aura of exclusively male society, in which the reigning symbols were distinctly macho—including the cigars.

If any of Mark Twain's houses resembled a steamboat, it was the place in Redding, Connecticut, called Stormfield, a great white structure perched like a beached ark on a hilltop. Named for the Captain of the *Extracts* (who was modeled after Mark Twain's friend Captain Ned Wakeman), it was nautical in spirit as well as shape, having been designed as a refuge in which to escape the press of the world—and the world press. But its name proved to be paradoxically prophetic, for the winds of winter howled like vengeful furies about the exposed building, and the isolation of the place turned out to be more lonely

than grand. Like Huck Finn on Jackson's Island, Mark Twain grew tired of his own company, and when he could not entice visitors to Stormfield, he paid visits elsewhere. Unlike the Hartford house, Stormfield was not Mark Twain's creation, but was the work of others, chiefly its architect, John Howells—son of William Dean. Yet in the end it proved to be a perfectly suitable setting for

Mark Twain's last years, less a floating palace than a ship of folly manned by a skeleton crew. Born in a rented shack, Mark Twain ended his life in an equivalent structure, like the Great Gatsby never more than a tenant in another man's mansion, rattling around in its vast unoccupied spaces like a weary ghost. He was dead before the greenery had really begun to grow.

We must distinguish once again, however, between appearance and reality, for in letters and in conversation Mark Twain declared himself delighted with Stormfield. "It is a perfect house—perfect, so far as I can see, in every detail," Paine reports him as saying. "It might have been here always." And Paine insists that "he was at home there from that moment—absolutely, marvelously at home, for he fitted the setting perfectly, and there was not a hitch or flaw in his adaptation." A young lady friend of those days, Elizabeth Wallace, tells us that Mark Twain refused to hang pictures on his walls, preferring to enjoy the natural gallery provided by his windows, and he wrote her describing the "autumn splendors" of Stormfield:

It was heaven and hell and sunset and rainbows and the aurora, all fused into one divine harmony, and you couldn't look at it and keep the tears back. All the hosannahing and strong gorgeousnesses have gone back to heaven and hell and the pole now, but no matter: if you could look out my bedroom window at this moment, you would choke up; and when you got your voice you would say this is not real, this is a dream. Such a singing together, and such a whispering together, and such a snuggling together of cosy soft colors, and such kissing and caressing, and such pretty blushing when the sun breaks out and catches those dainty weeds at it. . . .

STORMFIELD consists of 248 acres of finely located land: — hilltop, meadow, pasture and woodland, — a large acreage suitable for cultivation. There are two fine brooks, one flowing through a deep gorge; both brooks contain trout, and one of them is famous as a trout breeding place. Beautiful views in every direction. Too much cannot be said of the charm and picturesqueness of this estate.

Stormfield is sixty miles from New York City, and three and one half miles from Redding station. The road to it is excellent.

The house has eighteen rooms, with five bath-rooms, large loggia, fine closets and butler's pantry. The rooms downstairs are: living room, 20x40; dining room, 18x22; billiard room, 20x20; owner's office, kitchen, laundry, servants' dining room, butler's pantry, telephone closet, billiard-lavatory and toilet, and various closets, etc.; also the large loggia, open in summer, closed with windows for sun parlor in winter.

The rooms upstairs are: loggia bed-room, 18x22, with sleeping balcony; six other large bed-rooms for owner and guests, with four bath-rooms; also four servants' bedrooms, with bath-room; large attic, many closets, etc.

The heat is supplied by a large Richardson & Boynton steam plant, with hot water generator attached. The house is very warmly built, and the steam plant is never required to work up to anything like its full capacity.

The light is supplied by an acetylene lighting plant with 100 lights, and is capable of supplying 200 lights.

The water is supplied from a spring of the purest quality, is never failing, and has a steady flow of 4,000 gallons per day. It is forced to the house from a stone and cement reservoir holding 8,000 gallons, by a No. 8 Rider-Ericcson engine. Two copper tanks of 1,000 gallons each, in the attic, give the direct pressure and supply.

There is a modern model ice-house with a capacity of 100 tons.

The combination barn and garage is 20x50 feet, with a loft for hay.

78

Mr. Clemens' Favorite View of His Home

MARK TWAIN'S HOME "STORMFIELD"
with its 248 Acres at Redding, Conn.
—For Sale—

Mr. WILLIAM DEAN HOWELLS IN "MY MARK TWAIN"
HAS THIS TO SAY:

"He showed his absolute content with his house, and that was the greater pleasure for me because it was my son who designed it. . . . It opened in the surpassing loveliness of wooded and meadowed uplands. . . . Truly he loved the place."

FROM HIS BIOGRAPHER,
Mr. ALBERT BIGELOW PAINE:

"It is as lovely a home, with as fair a prospect, as any in New England."

Miss Wallace detected a similarly sensuous note in the landscape, which had by her report "nothing abrupt or harsh in the undulating curves of its hills and valleys; with something maternal in its soft, full outlines—where it would seem a sweet and restful thing to lay one's tired body down and let this mother Earth soothe and enfold you." This was not quite what Mark Twain seems to have had in mind, singing his November song, but from whatever perspective Stormfield would have made a lovely tomb.

Where the Hartford house is of a piece and at peace with its surroundings, set down as it was in the Nook Farm compound of similar if more restrained statements of Gilded Age taste, Stormfield appears in pictures to have been suddenly, even violently, thrust upon the scenery, like the pleasure dome reared a decade later at San Simeon in California by the Kublai Khan of yellow journalism, William Randolph Hearst. Stormfield seems more a miniature world's fair than the actual dwelling of a human being, a marvel of the latest plumbing and electrical wonders, and as at Iranistan, the owner-proprietor was on perpetual exhibition. While avoiding the madding crowd, Mark Twain was always at home to a host of friends and acquaintances like Elizabeth Wallace, to whom he wrote letters describing the beauties of the place in seductive terms, prose with all the stylistic subtlety of a real-estate brochure.

The view *was* truly grand,

but the landscape around was also very empty,

and when the camera caught Mark Twain outside,

among the columns and balustrades,

the owner looks out of place,

just another tourist stopping by to get his picture taken.

"I thought you went to Redding," chided Howells, "to get rid of Mark Twain," for his friend persisted in courting the press. He also tried to get Howells to live near Stormfield, but had difficulty even getting him up from Boston for a visit. Still, Howells had a double duty to perform, Stormfield being also his son John's "triumph," and he eventually spent some time in the big "house that Jack built." One result was a touching series of photographs that emphasizes the tenuous tie between Mark Twain and his Italianate palace, for as the two old men stand stationary in front of Stormfield—Mark Twain looming above the diminutive Howells—the camera moves in closer to them while making a slow circle, and though the men grow in relative size, the effect of the movement is to carry them away from the building, so that in the last picture they are standing virtually in open space. Despite Howells's stolidity and Mark Twain's firm stance—aided by his walking stick—they seem somehow evanescent, weightless, the cane serving as both support and stage prop, like Prospero's wand, reminding us that all life is a show. For even the great house itself would soon disappear, burning to the ground like Iranistan, and all we have left of it and the man who lived and died there are photographs, black-and-white rectangles illumined with the illusion of real life.

The End

In Camera

Yet we know also that Mark Twain had good times at Stormfield, that if he resembled a ghost wandering about in his nightgown, it was the kind of ghost that Halloween is likely to produce, having a mischievous child inside. Howells recalled that he was awakened every morning by the sound of his name, and when he looked out of his door, "there he was in his long nightgown swaying up and down the corridor, and wagging his great white head like a boy that leaves his bed and comes out in the hope of frolic with some one." Mark Twain was a human diamond, whose facets could burn saintly white and sulfurous blue, and whose radiance and sparkle were increased not diminished by flaws. Anything, recorded Paine, was likely to happen in his company, and at any time: "He was not to be learned in a day, or a week, or a month; some of those who knew him longest did not learn him at all."

Paine, like Howells, observed the boyishness of the old man, who in the morning could dote on death and damnation in his writings, then at lunchtime be impatient to begin "the afternoon of play." His favorite diversions were billiards and cards, games that played skill against chance, and the same fatalistic old party who longed aloud for the grassy grave regarded the cloth of green with something less than stoic indifference. "He was not," wrote Paine in a classic understatement, "an even tempered player." Boy and man, Mark Twain was a terrible-tempered Mr. Bang when it came to losing games or money, and children like Dorothy Quick who were lured to the card table soon learned that the old gentleman regarded it as no place for child's play. "I was so sorry that I had to do that, dear heart," he would drawl ☞

☞   ☞   87

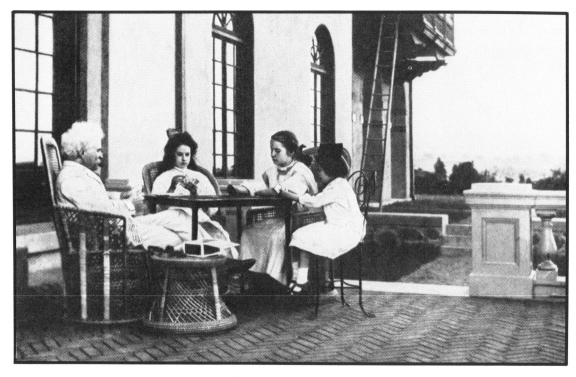

☞

with an uplifted eyebrow. "It just happened to be unavoidable."

Mark Twain in photographs likewise reflects a broad spectrum, ranging from stiffly somber to egregiously playful, yet he is seldom seen laughing, a strange omission for a professional (and private) funny man. Yet it is completely of a piece with his platform manner, his literary style, and his sense of self, for

his face was a mask that seldom varied from the expression worn here, along with a mourning band, by Mark Twain the grieving widower—a mood considerably enhanced by an unspeakably sober-sided Thomas Wentworth Higginson, biographer of Whittier and Longfellow and the improver of Emily Dickinson's verse.

Poker-faced, even glowering,

Mark Twain's scowling visage is stressed as his essential caricaturistic by every cartoonist who drew him. On the platform he wore the expression of a man on a gallows, and like sundry statesmen and criminals he preferred a serious mien for the photographic gallery: "I think a photograph is a most important document," he is quoted as saying by Elizabeth Wallace; "there is nothing more damning to go down to posterity than a silly, foolish smile caught and fixed forever."

In this he was of his own generation, the Brady bunch, who stared into the camera (or as here, away from it) as if it were the void of eternity, unwilling to be typed in amber with grins on their faces. In that first, braggadocio photograph with compositor's stick and ludicrous, hatlike pompadour (or pompadourlike hat), young Sam Clemens stares at the lens as down the barrel of a gun, with nervous eyes and a stiff upper lip. By 1870, when the budding author posed with two fellow journalists for this picture by Mathew Brady, the lip supported a stiff mustache that might occasionally add a droll line to his mouth but also swerved to screen any show of ivory. For Mark Twain was in the company of George Washington in one respect at least, the two of them having notoriously bad mouths, and even little Susy was forced to admit that her "extrodinarily fine looking" father did not have "extrodinary teeth."

And yet even today people seldom laugh or smile for a painted portrait, for the effect is usually dyspeptic. A smile is a spontaneous combustion, and must be caught in mid-wink to register as genuine and not as a grotesque, mortuary grin—the sort of instant reflex that only fast shutters and films can catch. Thus the daguerreotypers who replaced the itinerant limners of nineteenth-century America worked under conditions similar to painting, the long time exposures requiring a certain sobriety, often enforced by having the subject's head held in a clamp. Yet we cannot discount the eschatological factor also, for, as Mark Twain observed, the men and women of his generation regarded the taking of their pictures as a serious business. They dressed as for their funerals and customarily kept their tintypes stored in ornate, chambered albums resembling a family crypt.

Still, in the case of Mark Twain there are always exceptions, and when (as we shall see) he was once caught laughing, the results were happy. But in terms of numbers as well as numismatic poses, the published image of Mark Twain is overwhelmingly serious, a glowering phiz to which he gave humorous relief with well-chosen side effects. Along with funny hats and idiosyncratic cigar there was his academic robe, the wearing of which seems to have expressed a mingled mood of self-ridicule and pride, mockingly parading an honor that he earnestly courted and crossed the Atlantic to accept. "An Oxford decoration," he noted in his *Autobiography*, "is a loftier distinction than is conferrable by any other university on either side of the ocean, and is worth twenty-five of any other, whether foreign or domestic." It was with a similar mixture

of arrogance

and facetiousness

that he wore the Oxford gown, and though the honorary degree signaled Mark Twain's arrival at the top of the literary ladder, he persisted in behaving during the trip to receive it like the clown on the bottom rung. He paraded about London not in his academic garb but in his bathrobe, its color an electric blue, inspiring headlines, cartoons, and a despairing cable from Clara in America: "Much worried. Remember proprieties." The bathrobe and Clara's anguish were the harbingers of still another phase of Mark Twain's continuing performance, for his seventieth birthday had come and gone and the trouble had begun.

He called them his "granddaughters" at first, then institutionalized his girlish camp followers as the "Angel Fish," designating his billiards room where they gathered "The Aquarium." This piscatorial conceit Mark Twain brought back from Bermuda in 1908, a place where the days were forever fine for angel fish of whatever stripe. Elizabeth Wallace was witness to Mark Twain's Bermuda revels—though too old to participate in them—and reported in her diary (quoted by Hamlin Hill) that "if a child of ten or twelve happens to be anywhere within the radius of his glance he is inevitably sure of seeing her."

Then begins the most delightful flirtation. The King nods—if that is not effective he beckons with his hand and sometimes he goes up to the child and makes a remark that seems to continue a conversation broken off at some remoter period. He is nearly always sure to win their hearts and the most familiar sight is to see him playing cards or billiards with a Margaret or an Irene or a Dorothy.

His secretary testified also that Mark Twain's "first interest when he goes to a new place is to find little girls," whereupon "off he goes in a flash" in pursuit of "a new pair of slim little legs . . .

and if the girl wears butterfly bows of ribbon on the back of her head then
his delirium is complete."

As he had earlier picked a kitten to match his gray suit, Mark Twain instructed his little girl friends to wear white to go with his own, the child and the old man providing a veritable allegory of Cleanliness next to Godliness. "I prefer to be clean in the matter of raiment," he wrote in his autobiography, "clean in a dirty world." And yet William Dean Howells twitted his friend by calling him a "whited sepulchre," and his jests were seldom mere jokes. Many old men do take to pinching young arms and bottoms, and not all the Angel Fish were happy about joining the famous writer's school. Gershon Legman, who has made a profession of such matters, considers Mark Twain's attraction to "underage girls" evidence of sexual impotence, being otherwise "as ununderstandable as it is unsavory." Hamlin Hill also suspects a sinister dimension and reports a bit of gossip about "something very terrible that happened in Bermuda shortly before M.T.'s death," but whatever happened was "something unprintable" (according to his source) and hence not recorded. Whether or not Mark Twain pulled an equivalent performance to his act in Congress, we will never know, but certain it is that his proximity to little girls strikes the modern eye as strange.

To his contemporaries like Elizabeth Wallace, however, it seemed rather charming, this famous old gentleman cultivating the acquaintance of little girls, and mothers pushed their darlings upon him as if he were a Hollywood director. Which, in a sense, he was, arranging himself and child for the benefit of photographers for whom the arrangement was a picturesque study in whiteness and purity, the sexlessness of old age in company with the un- (or uni-) sex of childhood. Miss Wallace was the dean (i.e., warden) of women at the

University of Chicago, and one would think her suspicions would have been roused had there been anything untoward in the relationship. Yet she not only approved of the goings-on but wrote a little book about it for the unfortunate children who missed the show, *Mark Twain and The Happy Island* (1913). The book contains an approving preface by Albert Bigelow Paine, who himself posed his daughters in snug company with the old man and who treated the Angel Fish in his biography of Mark Twain as a delightful and innocent phenomenon.

But in the lower depths a few sharkish reservations are found lurking. In print both Miss Wallace and Paine explained that the little girls were surrogates for the dead Susy, yet Hill quotes a letter to Miss Wallace from Paine warning that the live Clara did not want published "any *'affectionate'* photographs" of Mark Twain "with young girls," and none appeared in *Happy Island*. Still, according to one of the Angel Fish, Dorothy Quick, her memories of life in the Aquarium were enchanting only, her recollected image of Mark Twain one of saintly Old Age: "I always associate him with brightness and cheer. The sun shining on his bright hair, outlining his figure as he walked, bringing out the lines life had destined him to wear—always the sunlight illuminating the days I spent with him." In short, a transcendentally clean old man, Hyperion once again, not a satyr, enveloped in a transfiguring cloud of glory. Yet it is such a light as deepens rather than dispels dark, and the little girls in attendance share his shadow.

Village
Queens

CHAPTER 10

Whatever else they were, the Angel Fish that swam through Mark Twain's last years are recognizable as a late manifestation of his persistent love affair with girlhood. On his rite of passage to Europe aboard the *Quaker City* in 1868, the young reporter from California divided his time between the matronly Mrs. Mary Fairbanks, whose censure in terms of manners and literary style he courted, and a girl named Emma Beach who was about half his age— seventeen. And it was on that same trip, according to his own handmade legend, that he first saw a picture of Olivia Langdon, who would become his wife and mother. "She was," he recalled in his *Autobiography*, "slender and beautiful and girlish—and she was both girl and woman. She remained both girl and woman to the last day of her life." Sixteen, he ruminated elsewhere in the same book, is the "dearest and sweetest of all ages." A projection of his own puerility (his wife called him "Youth"), Mark Twain's obsession gave life to his arch Becky Thatcher and is responsible also for his saintly Joan, the first a tribute to the girl he loved when a boy, the last an attempt to memorialize his favorite daughter as a maiden without peer. It was also responsible for the scorn Mark Twain would heap upon the doctrine of Immaculate Conception—which he seemed to take personally—yet it was accepted by his readers, who regarded perpetual girl-and-boyhood as a very nice idea, set to the tune of "Down by the Old Mill Stream."

In the European notebook-diary that contributed to *A Tramp Abroad*, Mark Twain recorded a boat trip down the Neckar that became an extended and elaborate "raft" voyage in the finished book. The diary version involves a running joke regarding the parties of little girls seen bathing along the riverbanks, "with an old mother in charge," which swell from twelve in number to twenty and then on to twenty-five as the boat descends the river. With Mark Twain perhaps more than with any other American writer, the line between fact and fiction, remembrance and wish fulfillment is almost nonexistent, so that even in his notebooks one cannot tell where record ends and invention begins. But one suspects that the increase in numbers of naked little girls is a result of Mark Twain's love of burlesque (in the literary sense), and this is most certainly the case when he notes that "H went swimming above where [the] 25 girls were & was warned away." Not only is H a fictional foil, added to the finished book as Harris, but the incident turns on the Victorian superstition concerning intrafluvial pregnancy.

Whether observed reality or fiction, none of the humorous elements survived the transition to published book. There the naked little girls are generalized as one "joyous group of naked children, the boys to themselves and the girls to themselves, the latter usually in the care of some motherly dame who sat in the shade of a tree with her knitting. The little boys swam out to us, sometimes, but the little maids stood kneedeep in the water and stopped their splashing and frolicking to inspect the raft with their innocent eyes as it drifted by." No mention is made of the boys in Mark Twain's notebook, and they were either added from memory or out of prudery, in either case as camouflage to avoid the charge of prurience. Much the same thing happens with a brief notation concerning a "slender naked girl" found bathing in the Neckar, who "snatched a leafy bough of a bush across her front and then stood satisfied, gazing out upon us as we floated by—a very pretty picture." As with the groups of little girls, this solitary September Morn becomes in the book a much more ornate arrangement:

Once we turned a corner suddenly and surprised a slender girl of twelve years or upward, just stepping into the water. She had not time to run, but she did what answered her just as well; she promptly drew a lithe young willow bough athwart her white body with one hand, and then contemplated us with a simple and untroubled interest. Thus she stood while we glided by. She was a pretty creature, and she and her willow bough made a very pretty picture, and one which could not offend the modesty of the most fastidious spectator. Her white skin had a low bank of fresh green willows for background and effective contrast—for she stood against them—and above and out of them projected the eager faces and white shoulders of two smaller girls.

The original notation is hardly erotic, but the fully developed picture noisily places a skirt of propriety (and escort-companions) around the central figure, thereby making it (and the book) suitable for a Victorian parlor, recognizable as one of the sentimental tableaux, the *Kindern Kitschen* that passed for art in 1880.

Gershon Legman tells us that dirty jokes are self-revealing, and a psychologist might say that in his Neckar burlesque Mark Twain was stripping himself naked also, H being a self-projection engaged (and thwarted) in an act of wish fulfillment. Harris acts as something of an alter ego in the book, and *H* is an autobiographical initial, from Hannibal to Hadleyburg to Heidelberg and on to Huck and Jesus H. Christ Himself—the model in the early notebooks for Little Satan, the Mysterious Stranger. And the bough screening the young maiden, like the bow of Diana bathing, may be read as a defense mechanism—though rooted in reality—being psychic camouflage to protect the viewer, lest he like Actaeon be torn to pieces. Similarly, in the matter of the Angel Fish, Mark Twain took care that the relationship remained above reproach, that it was "one which could not offend the most fastidious spectator." By tracking backward to the naked girls along the Neckar, we may by implication strip the later relationship of the sentimental persiflage with which Mark Twain draped it.

And yet there are any number of explanations other than sexual for Mark Twain's attraction to little girls—which, after all, included his own daughters. He himself said that having reached a grandfatherly age and being without grandchildren, he decided to adopt some, an explanation that has a psychological dimension also. For as Hamlin Hill has shown us, during this period Clemens' daughters were increasingly estranged from him and seemed ungrateful and selfish. By taking on the "adopted" grandchildren, he delivered a double rebuke, both for their failure to get married and have children of their own and for neglecting their father. Thus the Angel Fish were "grand" children, not mean and spiteful ones. Certain it is that the old man was terribly lonely in his last years and kept Paine up all hours of the night playing billiards and feeding his vanity. By cultivating other people's little girls, Mark Twain sought to fill that particular vacuum also, for they provided the kind of companionship that came thickly spread with the "butter" (as he called it) of adoring flattery that the girl children of Victorian households were trained to deliver by the pound.

Among the amusements shared by Mark Twain and his Angel Fish was a

game Dorothy Quick called "skeleton signatures," played "by folding a sheet of paper in half, then straightening it out and writing one's name on the crease, then quickly folding the paper together again and rubbing it on the outside so that the ink would blot. The result was a skeleton-like figure that was invariably amusing." Mark Twain preferred to call the game "ghosts," because the figures "were very wraith-like and ethereal looking," and though the game is now played in psychiatrists' offices, it still turns on the relativity of appearances. Inkblots like "ghosts" are a tenuous matter, a game at which any number can play, and bestiality like beauty is in the eye of the beholder, who may do what he will with white dresses and black stockings. Mark Twain seems to have found in kittens the same fresh-faced innocence he valued in little girls, yet the psychosexual commentators have remained silent (at this writing) concerning his relationship with cats.

The little girls, finally, are what you wish to make of them, and where Mark Twain's contemporaries recognized a familiar and sentimental grouping, modern eyes see something strange but equally familiar, Humbert Humbert *déjà vu,* the butterfly man embracing his butterfly girl. Something similar happens to an innocent remark by Elizabeth Wallace, who in speaking of Mark Twain's fondness for billiards, declares that "it was a pretty sight to see him teaching his little girl friends to play, and encouraging them by letting them beat him." For it all belongs to a different century, in the dim regions of weird explored by Sigmund Freud, where all fades except the final question. What we are left with are merely pictures, which do not lie only because they cannot talk. The point to be made here is that as sentimental posturing or sublimated sex they are pure theater, nascent Hollywood, part of the changing obscenery we call entertainment. We will never know the facts of the matter, and it is best to deal with the Fish as with the Suit and the Houses, in terms of symbols, thereby attaining a larger and even literary truth. And as literature, the Angel Fish are most meaningful when returned to Bermuda, where Mark Twain found so many of the tribe, there to figure in a drama starring a Prospero who may have been a Caliban in disguise, but who kept the lecherous traitor within held firmly in check.

The Bermuda Triangle

Like Hannibal and Heidelberg, the Happy Island was one of Mark Twain's particular places. As a young man, in 1877, he had traveled to Bermuda with his boon companion, the Reverend Joseph ("Joe") Twichell, a liberal-minded minister from Hartford who played Nigger Jim to Mark Twain's Huck in several of his literary journeys. That Bermuda jaunt, Mark Twain noted in his diary, was the "first actual pleasure trip I ever took," and he wrote afterwards to Joe that "it was much the joyousest trip I ever had . . . not a heartache in it, not a twinge of conscience." Like the "raft" tour down the Neckar, in which Mark Twain was joined once again by Twichell, the Bermuda sojourn was one of the many autobiographical incidents that eventually flowed marvelously together as the adventures of Huckleberry Finn. For like the Hannibal Arcadia, the Bermuda idyll was the stuff of which nostalgic reminiscence is spun.

When Mark Twain returned to Bermuda nearly thirty years later, in 1906, he took Joe Twichell with him again, but the formerly charming companion proved to be a terrible bore. Mark Twain's last journey to Hannibal, in 1902, was similarly disillusioning, reminding the author not so much of his childhood as of his old age, for the place had become the kind of garden in which Death chiefly dwells: "Almost every tombstone recorded a forgotten name that had been familiar and pleasant to my ear when I was a boy there fifty years before." Reunited for the moment with his old girl friend, Laura Hawkins, who had served as the model for Becky Thatcher, Mark Twain discovered that she had put on more than years. Thenceforth he associated himself with less substantial (but no less substantive) symbols of corporeal innocence, commencing with his participation in the Hannibal High School graduation exercises, where the famous author found himself seated "at the base of a great pyramid of girls dressed in white."

Like Dorothy Wordsworth in her brother's "Lucy poems," the many maidens gathered to Mark Twain's aging bosom were the kinds of butterflies that suggest emblems of psyche or soul. Lewis Carroll kept the Wordsworthian tradition alive during the Victorian age in Great Britain, stalking soulful little

girls with gumdrops and camera, but it was Mark Twain who gave an American dimension to what had been up to then a distinctly English obsession. Where Wordsworth resigned himself to the consolations of philosophy, where Carroll became an artful Dodgson, Mark Twain tried to do what Tom Wolfe (the Elder) said could not be done—he tried to pull himself through the knothole of lost time. Whether the Angel Fish were tokens of his childhood or surrogates for his little girl lost, they add up to a potent metaphor, being very real children who obliged the great author by putting on old-fashioned costumes. As Susy, Clara, and Jean had acted out *The Prince and the Pauper* in home theatricals, so Mark Twain's "granddaughters" trooped across the stage of his private fantasy world by becoming virginal versions of American girlhood and particular mementos from Mark Twain's past, a series of Orphan Annies come to visit.

Because the published record emphasizes the Bermuda backdrop to this pastoral masquerade—thanks to Elizabeth Wallace's efforts—added complexity is suggested by the looming presence in *Mark Twain and The Happy Island* of Henry Huttleston Rogers, the shrewd and powerful Standard Oil executive who was Mark Twain's personal $avior. Having helped the author recover his fortune and preserve his good name, Rogers was rewarded for his efforts by undying loyalty and unremittent kidding, a tension between love and competitiveness which was Mark Twain's way of dealing with male affection. It is a manner familiar to natives of New England like Rogers, who not only enjoyed the sport but joined in the fun as well, and the two old men spent their season in paradise (in 1907) playing hearts and exchanging insults, much to the delight of Mark Twain's little girl friends and their mothers. When out walking, Rogers

maintained a slow and majestic gait,

in keeping with his large and portly frame,

turning his head and looking about him as he advanced. "There he comes," Mark Twain would cry to his giggling audience, "looking just like Gibbs' Lighthouse, stiff and tall, turning his lights from side to side!" Called King by his young friends and other admirers, Mark Twain "hit upon the happy idea of calling Mr. Rogers the Rajah," and the old pirate (as Mark Twain also called him) played Jolly Rajah to Mark Twain's Merry Monarch.

But the two old men, each picturesque in his own way, seem somehow anomalous in Bermuda: attended by fairylike little girls in white pinafores, they are, like Bottom in fairyland (or Satan in Eden), completely out of place. In pictures together they resemble aging birds of prey, Brer Vulture and Brer Hawk; and this sinister dimension darkens further when one realizes what went on beyond the camera and out of reach of biographers, reporters, and little girls. For aboard Rogers' luxurious yacht *Kanawha* ("fastest in American waters") it was Rabelais who was the reigning genius, and "roger" took on yet another punning sense—albeit remaining "stiff and tall." Only small crumbs remain of those profane feasts, like the burlesque poem called "The Mammoth Cod," which Gershon Legman has mounted as positive evidence of Mark Twain's impotence and which certainly testifies to his dirty mind. For whatever else it may be, Mark Twain's "Cod" is a clue to the goings-on in the *Kanawha*'s main cabin, which was little different from the rough male humor that held forth in the miners' shacks and shanties where Mark Twain had lived—and learned—nearly fifty years before.

The presence of these two old rogues amid the admiring little girls and their mamas on Bermuda is somehow reminiscent of the rascally King and

113

Duke in the heart of the Wilkses' home in *Huckleberry Finn*. The oldest of the Wilks girls, Mary Jane, is one of Mark Twain's sterling heroines, a nineteen-year-old redhead who is "sweet and lovely" but also full of "sand" (i.e., true grit). Adored by Huck Finn, she serves as innocent foil to the two swindlers, her goodness making them all the worse. Though the contingency was hardly conscious, the fact remains that during the decade when Mark Twain was writing his darkest and most despairing works, identifying himself with the incarnate principal of evil, he traveled to the Edenic "Happy Island" and ingratiated himself with the most vibrant symbol of innocence available. So Satan is drawn to Eve for other reasons than sex, and Claggart plays symbolic court to Billy Budd, a sinister magnetism that is central to the mystery of iniquity, a lust that is finally philosophical, whatever its psychological base.

The contrast between Mark Twain and the little girls with whom he posed is one of those duplicitous dimensions engendered by the Gilded Age, which produced a public literature that was gelded and private works like "The Mammoth Cod." Mark Twain likewise comported himself with decent restraint in the company of men he loathed, delivering humorous tributes to such as Andrew Carnegie even as he flayed the cherubic capitalist at his leisure in the dark dungeon of his *Autobiography*. We may if we wish conjure up an alternative version of this situation, relying for content upon Mark Twain's secret eruptions, but the result, even to modern sensibilities, is intolerable, for in life as in literature certain decorums must be observed. Like Mark Twain in his coffin, these matters remain a mystery, to which the photographic and written records provide no key. Let us leave him then as he wished to be remembered, in his white suit surrounded by little girls in butterfly bows. Sentimental as anything dreamed up by Emmeline Grangerford, it is also sinister betimes, a study in absolutes resembling Robert Frost's poetic "Design." Providing no answers, it leaves us with a question that verges on the nothingness from which Mark Twain addressed his last great work, that masterpiece of mutability, his *Autobiography*, an album stuffed with pictures of the dead taken by a "mental camera" that is now a skull.

I have been chief guest at a good many banquets myself, and I know what brother Andrew is feeling like now. He has been receiving compliments and nothing but compliments, but he knows that there is another side to him that needs censure.

I am going to vary the complimentary monotony. While we have all been listening to the complimentary talk Mr. Carnegie's face has scintillated with fictitious innocence. You'd think he never committed a crime in his life. But he has.

Look at his pestiferous simplified spelling. Imagine the calamity on two sides of the ocean when he foisted his simplified spelling on the whole human race. We've got it all now so that nobody could spell. . . .

If Mr. Carnegie had left spelling alone we wouldn't have had any spots on the sun, or any San Francisco quake, or any business depression.

There, I trust he feels better now and that he has enjoyed my abuse more than he did his compliments. And now that I think I have him smoothed down and feeling comfortable I just want to say one thing more—that his simplified spelling is all right enough, but, like chastity, you can carry it too far.

117

Yes and I read in the papers that Judge Kenesaw Mountain Landis fined Standard Oil nearly thirty million dollars for violating the Elkins act, and here the President of the United States is doing the same thing to the Senate, for free. Well, it reminds me of what the bride said the morning after: "I expected it but didn't suppose it would be so big." Which brings me to the subject of Andrew Carnegie . . . because he is so small, that is . . . in stature, I mean. Andrew always recalls to my mind the man who was so short the doctor couldn't tell whether he had a sore throat or piles. Whenever I see Andrew I remember a lawyer I once knew, a legal midget who was famous for two things, his short size and a prosecution complex. When he got through with a witness there was nothing left of that witness, more or less like the German language and a cat. The Germans take a cat, and start her in at the nominative singular in good health and fair to look upon and then they sweat her through all the four cases, and when she limps out through the accusative plural, you wouldn't recognize her for the same being. Yes sir, once the German grammar gets hold of a cat, it's good-bye cat. And that's the way this little lawyer was when it came to cross-examining witnesses. It was said that when he got through with a witness there was nothing left but a limp and defeated and withered rag. Except once. Just that one time the witness did not wither. The witness was a vast Irishwoman and she was testifying in her own case. The charge was rape. She said she awoke in the morning and found the accused lying beside her, and she discovered that she had been outraged. The lawyer said, after elaborately measuring her great figure impressively with his eye, "Now Madam, what an impossible miracle you are hoping to persuade this jury to believe! If one may take so preposterous a thing as that seriously, you might even charge it upon me. Come now, suppose you should wake up and find me lying beside you? What would you think?" She measured him critically and at her leisure, with a calm, judicious eye, and said, "I'd think I'd had a miscarriage!"

Now I hope that story didn't offend any of you. I have nothing against miscarriages, and number several among my acquaintants. Why there was a woman in Duluth who had a miscarriage once and left town immediately thereafter, but when she came back thirty years later it was running for Congress. And speaking of congress, I am reminded of the man who thought he had courted a virgin until the wedding night, when he found an advertisement for a gonorrhea cure stenciled on her stomach. . . . .

We cannot forget the other Mark Twain, the ranting rascal with the ubiquitous cigar, not only because he is part of the whole but because, as Albert Bigelow Paine long ago said, he is part of us all. Taken together, the various versions of Mark Twain old provide a perilous balance that threatens to break into sudden movement, much as the man and his fictions provide an unstable, hence kinetic, unit. That is, finally, the power and the mystery of Mark Twain as eidolon, for as Kineman he is not one but many images, pictures on a whirling disc that merge in the illusion of motion and life. What follows are several series of those moving pictures, studies in complements and contrasts that certify the bond between art and fact, becoming the kinds of artifact that so often for Mark Twain turn on a most singular first person.

By chance at least four of the violets that kept company with the mossy old stone were named Dorothy, and the foremost as well as the first of these was Dorothy Quick. Eleven years old when she met Mark Twain, she was a not-so-little girl—"big for my age" as she put it—and with a curiously adult set of features. Hers was a face that, like her marvelous name, could have come out of any Victorian children's book illustrated by Sir John Tenniel. And when she undertook a half-century later to write up her memories in a book called *Enchantment*, she compared herself to Lewis Carroll's Alice, stepping through "the mirror of the present into the past and living days that were full of joy and color." Not that her days with Mark Twain resembled a surreal drama on the far side of a fun-house mirror, quite the opposite, for his proximity provided "a rarefied atmosphere in which all things of life seemed to assume their true and proper proportions." At times Dorothy's recollections seem too good to be true, for as literature they recall *Happy Island*, being an atavistic exercise in turn-of-the-century sentimentalism. And like Miss Wallace, Dorothy illustrated her recollections with photographs, though in this case she is the only Angel Fish in the tank.

Unlike Miss Wallace, however, she included in her book photographic displays of affection—for true to her name, Mistress Quick nimbly leapt into Mark Twain's lap—and she thereby ignored the injunction of Clara Clemens, who died the following year. Dorothy's book was hardly responsible for Clara's demise, yet the conjunction is symbolic, the pictures somehow breaking a spell and withering the wicked witch. And it is Dorothy of Kansas that Mistress Quick most closely resembles, not Alice in Wonderland, for Mark Twain

CHAPTER 12

The
Wizard
of Ooze

played a role in her young life similar to that of the Wonderful Wizard, being an object of veneration and pilgrimage who works a marvelous transformation. Like the Wizard, also, Mark Twain remained something of a cipher, even a sham, and though Dorothy sought him out, it was because he needed her, being in truth a combination Scarecrow, Tin Man, and Cowardly Lion. She filled a vacant place in the region of his heart, yet was never anything more than a substitute, much as her adoration of Mark Twain was more oleo than butter. Like any kitten, she knew how to retain a comfy lap, and added hers to the warm bath of caressing tongues that washed Mark Twain in his clean old age.

It may be truly said that what the aging author wanted he got, and if it did not bring him final happiness, the fault cannot be laid to those around him. Save for his daughters, Clara and Jean, who were seldom nearby, Mark Twain was surrounded by kind hearts and gentle hands that rocked him as in a cradle or casket toward the grave. The pictures of Dorothy Quick and Mark Twain almost dead are integral to this final stage of his life, being an important part of the drama as he wished it to be played, Cordelia reunited with Lear, and it was in a similar capacity that Dorothy herself wanted to be remembered. In the photographs she selected for her book, Dorothy appears in a protective posture, whether sitting in the foreground, placed between Mark Twain and the camera, or perched in such a way that her head is higher than his. As we shall see, other positions were captured on film that emphasize a somewhat different relationship, but *Enchantment* for Dorothy was a giant doll named Mr. Clemens—or SLC, as she came to call him. As the taking of the photographs lends a consistent pattern—even a plot—to Dorothy's memories, so the fact of them provides a complex symbol, much as the book in which they appear is really a photograph album with extended notes, an anatomy whose focus is Mark Twain. Along with *Happy Island* Dorothy's *Enchantment* provides counterpoise to the encyclopedic *Autobiography*, and though none of the three books is trustworthy, all are indispensable, being the final chapters in a life that, from the outset, melded fact into a dominating frame of fiction.

The friendship between Dorothy and Mark Twain began aboard the S.S. *Minnetonka*, homeward bound from England, where the famous author had been to receive his Oxford degree. It was for the old man an ego trip, an absolute exercise in vanity, which Dorothy kept moving as they walked the decks, by describing to Mark Twain "the parts I liked best" in his books. For her good work she received a suitable reward and was allowed to choose one of many "photographs of him in all his favorite poses that were already familiar to me." All were "splendid and life-like, for Mark Twain always photographed exceedingly well," and with admirable self-restraint, well-mannered Dorothy picked out a small "head study." But the great man was aggrieved that she hadn't picked "one in my white suit," but had chosen "the smallest of them all," and in the end Dorothy got to keep her first choice and was given a full-length photo as well.

It was not long before she began to find herself posing for photographs with Mark Twain at the request of passengers, and when she was asked to add her autograph to his famous scrawl, Dorothy felt "very important." Dorothy had her own small measure of vanity and seems to have been aware from the beginning that hers was not a friendship with just any old man, an impression borne out when the ship docked in New York. What had gone on before aboard the *Minnetonka* "was nothing to the orgy" of picture taking that took place as reporters swarmed aboard with their cameras "all ready to be focused on Mark Twain." Gallant gentleman that he was, Mark Twain insisted that she be in those pictures too, and the following day "there was not a paper in New York . . . that didn't carry a photograph of 'Mark Twain and Dorothy Quick.' " Whatever the psychological attraction between the old man and the young girl, it was a mutual appetite thenceforth where pictures and publicity were concerned, and Dorothy's friendship with Mark Twain became the kind that warmed George Eastman's heart. Happiest when basking in the reflections from his old glory, Dorothy liked to have it down in black and white, and whenever she paid Mark Twain a visit, she took care to pack a Brownie in her bag.

She first came to call at his rented house in Tuxedo Park, and what went on there is suggested by the title of her Chapter Nine: "We Eat Plums and Take Pictures." The word "kodak" was for Mark Twain the stylistic purist an acceptable verb, and he and Dorothy kodaked each other "on the porches and in the garden by the nasturtiums. Later we even made what Mr. Clemens christened 'hunting expeditions,' because we did literally hunt for backgrounds." This was not difficult, for "all the Park was a picturesque landscape," but Dorothy had particular memories of being kodaked atop a fieldstone gatepost, Mark Twain "taking a great deal of care that my long braids should be at just the right angle." The euphoria of life in Tuxedo Park was disturbed only when they ran out of film after the stores were closed, but Dorothy was consoled by Mark Twain's promise that he would take her to the village in the morning "to

Just after our friendship began,
Mark Twain and I posed
for photographers on board
the "S.S. Minnetonka."

This photograph of us, taken
on the side porch of Mark
Twain's home in Tuxedo Park,
was his favorite.

Mark Twain in his beloved Oxford gown. I always wore his favorite white when I visited him.

buy another roll and get these developed, and if they don't come out, we'll take some more."

At night, when the available light was inadequate for kodaking, Mark Twain and Dorothy would relax and listen to his orchestrelle, which as a mechanical marvel was a cross between incidental entertainment and actual function, the musical equivalent of the Paige Typesetter. When operating, the orchestrelle resembled a Hammond Organ in that it was a reasonable facsimile of several instruments playing at once. But unlike the Hammond, it required no skill to operate, only endurance, for in the manner of a player piano it worked from rolls and was powered by pedals—which is to say feet. Mark Twain's Hammond was his typewriter, which was organ enough for him, and though he liked to pound out the piano accompaniment to his own rendition of Negro spirituals, he preferred to listen, not work, when the orchestrelle was playing. Thus the chore often fell to his secretary, who would keep the organ going for hours as the King and young guest relaxed to the eclectic strains of classical and modern music, including Wagner's "Wedding March" and "The Last Rose of Summer."

The evening concert was central to life as it was lived by Mark Twain in his last years, the old man sitting back in an overstuffed chair, pulling on one of his interminable cigars as "the wonderful music came flowing out into the room. At first it was like the gentle, peaceful waves that caress the beach; then, as the crescendo mounted, they became great breakers that pounded on the feelings, until one felt that they were caught up in the melody and swept into far, unknown lands wherein there was only beauty. That is the way Mr. Clemens later described it to me, and it was truly so." No better metaphor likewise could be found for the old man's easeful progress toward death, which like the "wonderful music" that came out of the marvelous machine was the footwork of Mark Twain's secretary, a transcendent variety of the species who not only kept her employer's secrets but sheltered him from all harsh and unpleasant truths— including his daughters.

It was Mark Twain's secretary who, besides carrying out the duties for which she had been hired (at fifty dollars a month, with board and room), ran his household, not only counting up the words he wrote—which at thirty cents each brought in the money that paid the bills—but paying the bills also, and it was she who, when errands needed to be run, ran them. When Mark Twain and Dorothy wanted to be kodaked together ("Try as we may," said SLC, "we've never been able to do that ourselves"), she was happy to oblige. It was she also who dressed Dorothy up for the camera one day as an Indian princess, with "elongated eyes, beaded lashes, and crimson mouth," draping her with "long turquoise chiffon veils . . . until I looked like a veritable rani of old India." And when, one evening, Mark Twain and Dorothy decided to start a butterfly collection, it was the secretary who braved the cold for an hour, catching moths attracted to the light on the porch. The secretary was also the one who warned Dorothy, following an unhappy episode during the great Moth Hunt, that Mark Twain the master of dialect "detested slang," and it was she who held the collective household breath when Dorothy in ignorance broke the shibboleth (and silence) concerning Christmas presents. In short, the secretary was a human version of the orchestrelle, whose motive power she provided, a combi-

127

nation of functions intended to produce unceasing harmony, a seven-day-a-week wonder whose name was Isabel Lyon—though you won't learn that from Dorothy Quick.

You won't, because when Dorothy's book was published, Miss Lyon was out of the official picture, much as she was cropped from a photograph of Mark Twain and Jean when it was published by Milton Meltzer in *Mark Twain Himself* a year before *Enchantment* appeared. Though she worked for Mark Twain from 1902 until 1909, becoming after Livy's death the most important woman in his daily life, Isabel Lyon became a *persona non grata* to the Clemens family thereafter. Having come afoul of the terrible-tempered old man and his daughter Clara, so long as Mark Twain's oldest daughter lived, Isabel Lyon remained a nonperson, a wrong that was ironically enforced by the secretary's refusal to right it so long as Clara remained alive. Even as late as 1965 Justin Kaplan prolonged the injustice by publishing a Clarafied version of what happened in 1909, and it was only in 1973 that Hamlin Hill finally set the record straight. Relying on Isabel Lyon's diary, Hill told a story kept hidden for more than half a century, one that is closer to the *Autobiography* in mood than to Dorothy's recollections. Yet it is a tale containing enchantment too, being something of a ghost story, the shades of the past summoned up to recount their fates, horrors beyond the range of any camera to catch.

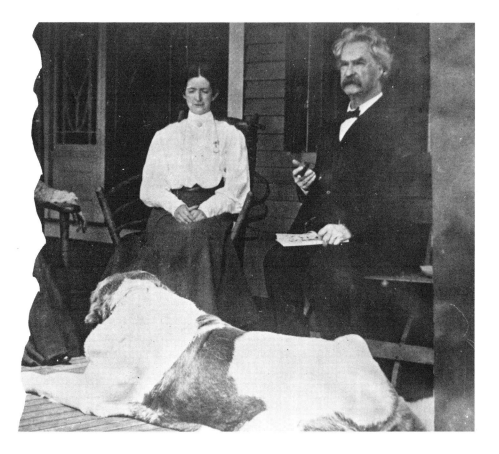

The Turn of the Shrew

CHAPTER 13

Isabel Lyon first joined the Clemens menagerie as secretary to Livy, a paradoxical circumstance given the eventual drama in which she played a definitive role; yet from first to last hers was a part for which she was in every way typecast. At age thirty-eight (in 1902) Miss Lyon was one of those spinsters produced in abundance in Victorian America as well as England, being a woman of talent, intelligence, and handsome features who for one reason or other had not found a husband and was forced therefore to find a place in someone else's family. She had been a governess along the way, and that soon enough became one of her many responsibilities in the Clemens household, where after Livy's death she played mother not only to the grown daughters but to that perpetual boy Sam Clemens. "Lioness" she was called in a home given to bestowing cute nicknames on people, and in terms of metaphor she played helpmate and mother to the king of an increasingly wild jungle. Not surprisingly, Isabel at times entertained hope of marriage to her "master" (as she called him), and in symbolic terms she did become a substitute wife, taking on a number of Livy's functions, but never the strategic one.

Wife without the sign, Isabel Lyon shared a spinster's fate with Emily Dickinson (as Mark Twain shared her costume), but in terms of literature she most closely resembles the unnamed governess in Henry James's *The Turn of the Screw*. In love with her employer, bedeviled by his children, and haunted by the ghosts of a dubious, even unnatural, relationship that did not end but was intensified by death—the memory of Susy, the perfect daughter, and Livy, the pluperfect wife—Isabel, like James's governess, began to suffer from the "nervousness" enjoyed by so many women of her period, and at times was confined by a paralytic hysteria. Yet she was an enormously energetic and enterprising person with vast powers of adoration where her irascible and unpredictable chief charge was concerned: "O Terrible," she wrote in her diary, "Terrible that his children cannot come under the spell of his glories, his subtleties, his sweetnesses. For this morning there was a cruel letter from Jean damning me—finding fault with him—with *him.*"

Jean's "cruel letter" was a manifestation of mental illness, for like Clara she was locked in a destructive embrace with her father, the exact nature of which we shall never know. But where Clara was normal in the eyes of the world, Jean was an epileptic, who suffered spells of depression and was subject to fits of violence—she once tried to kill Katy Leary, the Clemenses' beloved cook, and menaced Miss Lyon herself. Where Clara provided definable tensions in the home circle, Jean was a constant threat, and Isabel Lyon, whose every waking moment was devoted to protecting Mark Twain, saw to it that Jean was kept away in various asylums for many years. Unlike Clara, who herself sought to keep her distance, Jean was not happy in exile, hence the accusing letter, and it is not surprising that Isabel was especially fond of Clara, who was beautiful, talented, and away. But in the end it was she who proved to be the most terrible child of the two, at least in respect to Miss Lyon's fate.

In her desire to be helpful, in her devout wish to protect her master from all discomfort, Isabel Lyon set a Jamesian stage for a complex denouement, the kind in which the darkest beast springs from the jolliest corner. And the stage, as in so many stories by Henry James, took the outward form of a house, the Italianate villa called Stormfield, fit scene for a Jacobean drama. Though designed by John Howells, Stormfield was decorated within by Isabel Lyon, who was rewarded for this and her many other labors of love by the gift of a house of her own nearby, not a new but an old one, somewhat in need of repair. Both places were under construction at the same time, and in managing the accounts, Miss Lyon occasionally confused what was hers and what was Mark Twain's. The sums involved did not amount to more than a few thousand dollars, nor was there ever any proof of conscious wrongdoing on the secretary's part, whose confusion was another manifestation of what she thought was a close relationship with her employer. It was all understandable, but regrettable also, and a fatal mistake as things turned out. Miss Lyon called her own little nest the Lobster Pot, and it was like the bigger house ironically named. For as the winds of winter shrieked like furious ghosts about the new mansion on the hill, so the old cottage below became a trap, the Jamesian kind that betrays itself with a click only after you are inside. Soon enough the "dear weight of Stormfield," as she described it, would fall on Isabel Lyon like a ton of bric-a-brac and mortar.

Like one of James's heroines, Isabel suffered from illusions, for her love of Sam Clemens blinded her to certain dangers that her own experience should have warned her against, chief of which was the high mortality rate among those who involved themselves in his business dealings. The company of Mark Twain could be charming, even when he was sozzled with Scotch, but the Mark Twain Company was something else again, and few who entered that uncharming circle escaped without being badly burned. As Mark Twain's amanuensis for a time and as his sympathetic audience always, Isabel Lyon knew perfectly well what went on in his *Autobiography*, but being a Jamesian heroine, she probably thought that her own honesty, decency, and intensely loyal feelings would protect her from all harm. Like James's governess (and *his* Isabel) she was wrong; in fact, it was her very zeal to do right by her employer that finally sprang the trigger of the trap. Still, the final turning of the screw was not her direct doing, but was the work of Ralph Ashcroft, a Jamesian type even to name and nationality.

Ashcroft was an Englishman who first called Mark Twain's attention to himself because of his abilities as treasurer of the Plasmon Company, a health-food firm that replaced the Paige Typesetter as Mark Twain's ongoing folly during the last decade of his life. This was in 1904, and Ashcroft was soon acting as the author's business manager, for it was he who hit upon the happy idea of incorporating Mark Twain, thereby allowing him to protect his copyrights further. But like his employer, Ashcroft was an overreacher, and he extended his grasp too far when he convinced Mark Twain to sign over his power of attorney to himself and Miss Lyon. As a legal step it was perhaps warranted by the old man's increasing infirmity, but in effect it cut off the Clemens daughters without a cent. Whatever Ashcroft's intentions were—and there is no proof at all that he intended to swindle anyone—such an arrangement was not likely to please Clara, who may have disliked her father but did not mind his money, having floated her modest singing talents on the profits from his Mississippi River works.

Mark Twain signed the papers in question in 1908, when Clara was in Europe singing and swinging from the arms of several young musicians with foreign names. Miss Lyon was at the height of her domestic powers, busy decorating Stormfield and her own little house, and she seems at this time to have raised objections to Clara's scale of living and may have made some starchy comments regarding her accompanists (male). She certainly knew that Sam Clemens the master of dirty jokes kept a watchful and upon occasion wrathful eye on Clara's social life, the Lincoln of our Literature being a very Superior Father where his daughters' choice of companions was concerned. But Clara knew a thing or two about Sam Clemens also, and catching wind of Ashcroft's legal maneuvers, she took strategic steps, arranging through Henry H. Rogers to have the household accounts audited. When discrepancies were found, Clara hit high C (for "Cash"), the note she knew would set her father vibrating with rage.

For reasons that are not clear, though apparently (so she thought) for the added convenience of her employer, Isabel Lyon became Mrs. Ralph Ashcroft early in 1909, but what followed soon after was anything but a honeymoon. Though Mark Twain at first resented Clara's charges against the Ashcrofts, then resisted the necessity of taking action—ironically, he most valued the *man's* services—when Henry H. Rogers finally spoke, it was the voice of God, and the newlyweds were driven thunderously from the Stormfield grounds. To leave Mark Twain's good graces was to enter the fiery precincts of his *Autobiography*, and Isabel soon joined that unhappy throng. Having first cleared himself of any blame in the affair—he claimed he could not remember signing anything, and declared he must have been hypnotized by the evil Ashcrofts—Mark Twain put poisonous pen to paper, drafting a novella-length letter to William Dean Howells, a paranoiac epistle never intended for the mails and only lately opened.

In that document, which has not yet been fully published, Mark Twain characterized Isabel Lyon as a self-styled "Star of the Harem," who "would get herself up in sensuous oriental silken flimseys of dainty dyes, and stretch herself out on her bepillowed lounge in her bedroom, in studied enticing attitudes, with an arm under her head and a cigarette between her lips, and imagine herself . . . waiting for the eunuchs to fetch the Sultan; and there she would lie by the hour enjoying the imaginary probabilities." This refugee from a painting by Gérôme or a cigar box was the same woman described by Mark Twain in the same letter as "slender, petite, comely, 38 years old by the almanac, and 17 in ways and carriage and dress," an arrested Becky Thatcher become a repulsive houri contemplating an unspeakable Arabian Night. "There is nothing about her," he went on to Howells, "that invites to intimate personal contact; her caressing touch—and she was always finding excuses to apply it—arch girly-girly pats on the back of my hand and playful little spats on my cheek with her fan—and these affectionate attentions always made me shrivel uncomfortably—much as happens when a frog jumps down my bosom. Howells, I could not go to bed with Miss Lyon, I would rather have a waxwork." She was, he declared, "an old, old virgin, and juiceless, whereas my passion was for the other kind."

This last demurrer, along with the pairing of the seventeen-year-old and the harem queen, is intriguing, for the girlish Isabel, transformed into the Jezebel of well-placed veils, is both counterpart and companion piece to Dorothy Quick's metamorphosis in the hands of the voluptuary in question. Most interesting, perhaps, is its irrelevance to the charges brought against

Isabel Lyon, which had nothing to do with sexual promiscuity. Mark Twain raised his shaggy eyebrows to Howells over the time spent by Miss Lyon and Ashcroft "in her bedroom . . . and with the door shut!" but he also knew that the couple, once married, kept to separate bedchambers, and the two were never accused publicly of doing anything in private other than conniving to swindle their employer. Even those charges were eventually dropped, being largely suspicions without real substance, leaving Mark Twain with the sole felicity of his vicarious revenge, which in the outpouring of wrath took a curiously sexual turn, suggesting the release of tensions long held.

As for Clara, having secured her fortune, she married one of her accompanists and returned to Europe to spend more money. Miss Lyon gone, Jean returned home but only to die. At the end Mark Twain was left alone with Paine, who took Isabel's place at the orchestrelle but who wisely kept his distance from the account books. As the King's surviving consort, Albert knew better than to meddle in Mark Twain's business affairs, and though he moved his own family into one wing of Stormfield after the Ashcrofts departed, he never confused what was his with what was Mark Twain's—at least not until after the great man died. It was then that Paine's turn came to play a Jamesian role, becoming just such a guardian of famous papers who drives aspiring scholars to aspirin and even to drink.

Paine appears to have taken actual pleasure in Isabel Lyon's dismissal, the two of them having had a misunderstanding over their various claims in the concern that was decided in the secretary's favor. He was not therefore unwilling to keep the silence decreed by Clara, and though his biography devotes nearly five hundred pages to the period 1902–1909, the all-purpose secretary is mentioned only once by name. Paine obviously saw himself as a loyal retainer, a Kent in service to an aging Lear, but from our perspective he seems more an Oswald, steward to Goneril. Yet Paine, like Miss Lyon, was sincerely devoted to Mark Twain while he lived, and despite their jealous rivalry, they were alike in their high regard for the man they served. To Paine we owe the most formal and complete biography written by someone who knew Mark Twain personally, and Isabel preserved in her diary an informal but intimate account of the pleasure of the company she shared with Paine, playing Mrs. Thrale to the other's Boswell.

Like Paine, moreover, Isabel Lyon also left a photographic record of those years. If Paine was cameraman to the King, Miss Lyon was kodaker in residence, for as her diary provides a counterpart to Paine's biography—being a graphic account of the often petty miseries and manias that are filtered out of the official version of those years—so Isabel's candid shots complement Paine's formal pictures, providing an unbuttoned record of the passing scene. Until banker turned burglar and she was poor once more, Isabel took hundreds of photos of Mark Twain and the people around him, though the only ones published during her lifetime (and without credit) are the pictures illustrating Elizabeth Wallace's *Happy Island*. In toto, the effect as in any mass demonstration

Perfectly Candid

of ego is both stunning and stultifying. It is as if in feeding Mark Twain's vanity, Isabel Lyon were also satisfying not only her own but everyone's appetite for worship, serving as vicaress for the vast public desire to devour Mark Twain's image, which as eidolon approximated a sacramental wafer. Like most Americans, Isabel could not get enough of Mark Twain, but being in a position of privileged access, she could do something about it, with the result that the popular urge to look upon the man in white was concentrated in this one intense and high-strung woman.

For Isabel as for other amateurs, then and now, the camera was mostly a means of capturing a memory, setting down forever something otherwise lost— be it only a moment of time—a visual approximation of memoranda. Paine also operated from motives of preservation, but he was primarily a memorialist, a Daniel Chester French of film, and with other "art" photographers of the day, whether Steichen, Stieglitz, or Coburn, he borrowed to achieve that end from the craft of painting. Shaping his subject flatteringly, he selected a few from many pictures taken. Here, for example, we have a series of photographs presumably taken by Paine but never published, showing Mark Twain at his Dublin, New Hampshire, retreat, strolling,

standing still,

and posing with a kitten,

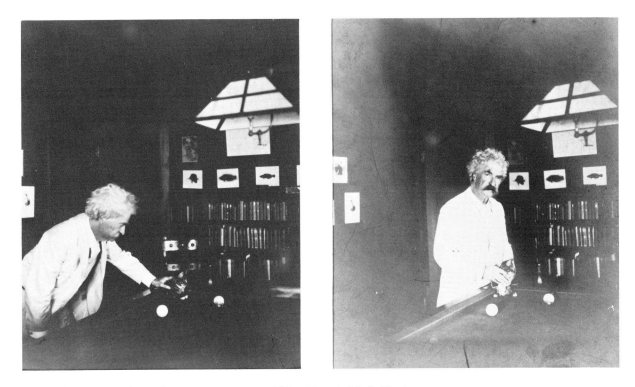

any one of which could stand the transition to marble. Here is Mark Twain
with billiard table and kitten, the "Aquarium" walls decorated with Angel Fish
of both kinds.

And here he is in the same setting with Louise Paine, the photograph of Dorothy as Indian princess discernible on the wall.

Each of these pictures, though informal in terms of content, is a sophisticated composition, like this photograph of Mark Twain studying an "arrangement" of billiard balls, whose placement cues a larger arrangement of triangles and rectangles.

143

But even the most careful photographer has to reckon (like the most skillful pool shark) upon the element of chance, a factor that distinguishes his craft from that of other graphic arts. Where the painter or sculptor generally strives to eliminate chance as a shaping force, keeping matters of design and composition completely under control, a photographer, even the most calculating artist, must come to terms with the large role played by chance in nature. Thus the landscape photographer is dependent on the vagaries of terrain, and though he may select a picturesque scene to frame on film, he is a lesser partner to the lay of the land, where the landscape painter, by contrast, may rearrange the scene to suit his aesthetic notions of beauty. A portrait in oils, likewise, is distinctly the creation of the artist, who may subtly select and alter reality in order to flatter a patron or severely portray the psychological truth he sees in the face before him. But the portrait photographer, while able to calculate certain final effects by mans of filters and lighting, must deal ultimately with factual, not abstract, features.

It is this matter of record, this absolute mirror likeness that the photographer's technology can capture more accurately than that of the most painstaking painter. Combined with cheapness, it resulted in the phenomenal spread of photography as a popular art form, and the earliest photographs, daguerreotypes, remain even now the most accurate likenesses ever taken. But to capture an accurate image is not the aim of the highest art, which tends ever toward abstraction. Great photographers have approximated great art in their work, but as artists they exercise most control after the picture is on film, whether by means of darkroom technology or, most important, in the process of selection.

By the former the photographer can imitate painterly effects—*vide* Coburn's misty versions of Mark Twain—but in the latter he must acknowledge the dominance of chance, especially in the case of portraits, for the most revealing picture is often one depending upon an accidental shift of eyebrow or posture, introducing an entirely unexpected but definitive dimension. "Taking" a picture is but the first step toward finding a telling image, which is more than a speaking likeness.

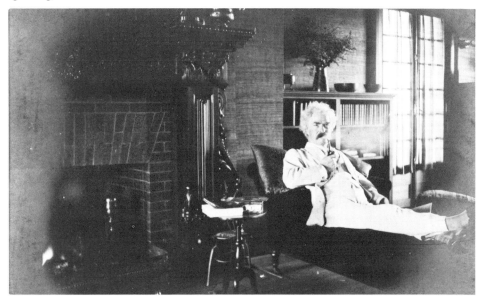

That is why the portrait photographer takes a number of exposures at one sitting, in the hope that one will correspond to his (or his customer's) notion of truth and beauty. We can see this demonstrated in reverse by the final frame of a series taken of Mark Twain (again presumably) by Paine in the Stormfield library, for the author's wary eye becomes a weary eye on the camera. In art photography such blunders are left on the darkroom floor, and this sequence was not published during Paine's long life. But in candid (or *en famille*) photography they are often of the essence, and what works against Paine's intention is precisely what we value in Isabel's informal shots. For spontaneity is here the ideal, a loose playing even dancing with chance, as in this picture from *Happy Island* which catches Mark Twain by surprise (but delighted), the shutter capturing him in the twinkle of a camera's eye. Like photos in any family album, these let us over the walls and into the home, conveying with force the man himself in an informal guise. "I've made some superb photographs of the King," exulted Miss Lyon in her journal in 1907, recording a triumph familiar to anyone who has ever taken pictures: "They are as active and as spirited as battleships."

Along with playing games of chance like "skeletons," Dorothy Quick and Mark Twain had fun picking out the "best" pictures from the ones they had taken. This is the finishing step to any photographic process, but what is often irritating to the artist is a matter of joy for the amateur, surprise over the unexpected pose or expression exploding in laughter. Dorothy remembered one picture in particular, in which Mark Twain's face was so shadowed that he "looked like a 'nice old white-haired nigger,'" as he colorfully put it, and it is this inadvertency of effect that lends to candid photography its peculiar grace note. Call it hazard, absurdity, what you will, the candid photograph lends to our perception of reality a new dimension, a higher visual order that only instant photography can provide. By framing it, the film lifts an unintentional (found) artifact into art, magnifying accident until it becomes icon.

Still, the dichotomy between art and amateur, posed and candid photography is not perfect. There is a middle range, a surreal zone, that we have only lately learned to appreciate. Thus the huge Saint Bernard in Paine's formal picture of Isabel, Jean, and Mark Twain adds another, unintended element to the

composition, and these two by Miss Lyon of Mark Twain confronting the automobile and the ocean have a similar quality, informality taking on the qualities of a new art form by asserting a new dimension of expression. "Candid," the kodak allowed for the kind of picture that could reveal the truth of a subject

caught off guard, but it was also *candide* in its effects, revealing the naïveté of the photographer by transcending, not destroying, the intended effect. It is a triumph not of technique but of technology, the sly wink of the shutter catching that most elusive of human expressions a laugh—a magic trick no artist's

150

pen or brush can duplicate—and often capturing and pinning to the wall even more ephemeral expressions. So the candid lens with the perfect innocence of the machine traps on film unexpected evidence of a circumstantial sort, and alongside the refreshing humor of Mark Twain loping along ahead of Henry Rogers, we have the much more ambiguous, though more carefully posed, pictures of the two old men. Again, where such accidents in traditional art are unwelcome specters—like double exposures—in candid photography they are the thing itself, and so instant photography becomes the reigning graphic form for an ephemeral age, and the candid camera, once the poor relation, becomes the missing, now the returned, heir of the world on celluloid film.

Mark Twain, as Dorothy Quick observed, was very photogenic, blessed with that elfskin glow that makes stars iridescent on film. But to be elfish is to cast a darker shadow also, and Mark Twain possessed another quality essential to Kineman, namely the mystery of duplicity, and in his pictures he conveys an impression of ambivalence that both enthralls and intrigues the viewer. Contemporary caricaturists and painters give us the most familiar image, the mask of Mark Twain the sulfurous saint, but it is the camera alone that conveys the subcutaneous elements of his make-up, catching glimpses of the uneasy eyes behind the face in its halo of hair. The camera, it is said, never lies, but that is because people do, and it is here finally that Isabel Lyon triumphs, for in bringing together Mark Twain and the camera—a union he devoutly desired—she effected an alchemical transformation of sorts, capturing Mercury, that illusive messenger, in her little black box. As with so many of Henry James's heavenly archers, the ultimate victory (though Pyrrhic) was hers.

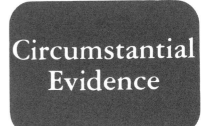

Circumstantial Evidence

Part Presbyterianism, part Pyrrhonism, Mark Twain's terminal pessimism was but a hardening of intellectual arteries, philosophical equivalent to the angina that crippled and then killed his physical self. His final view that "circumstance" was the ruling principal of the universe, that man was a victim of coincidences beyond his control, can be found expressed in his most affirmative fictions through the reticulations of plot. Whether in *Huckleberry Finn* or *The Prince and the Pauper,* events turn on hinges of circumstantial causality, coincidences involving withheld secrets, chance meetings, and the sudden reappearances of key characters and rafts. Artfully managed and sparingly used, as in the plays of Shakespeare and in Dickens' greatest novels, such devices can convey a sense of wonder, a marvelous element suggesting ultimate purpose (benign or malign) in the universe as well as revealing artistic design. In Mark Twain's fiction, however, these hinges of plot often shriek in outrage, being mostly strained arrangements of authorial convenience. A genius at improvisation, Mark Twain had a wooden hand, not a golden arm, when plotting his stories, and like Huck on the Mississippi, he tended to let things slide. Then, at the last, faced with the necessity of ending his narrative, he would bring in his Tom Sawyer half with a cliché bag of authorial tricks.

It is the Huck Finn side we prize most in Mark Twain, the easy vernacular flow of incident and episode epitomized by his *Autobiography*, that random, miscellaneous demonstration of perfect artlessness that is as reflective of mood and occasion as a woodland pool or a psychiatrist's couch. Still, we must acknowledge the Tom Sawyer part also, traces of which may be found throughout his notebooks, suggesting that the traps he used to catch his readers—and his characters—were essential to the man who created Huckleberry Finn. Tom's famous fence, the hoaxing dialogue with the pilot in *Life on the Mississippi*, the switched children and mixed identities in *Pudd'nhead Wilson* and *The Prince and the Pauper*, the prank that provides the plot of "The Man That Corrupted Hadleyburg," all the evidence adds up to the conclusion that *What Is Man?* was a loaded question, that Mark Twain's trickster God was a projection of himself. His love of impossible turns of plot seems part of his love of complicated gadgets—always his weak side—gismos and thingamabobs that went haywire the moment before a potential investor entered the room. Under this heading we may therefore include not only the typesetter and the orchestrelle but the notorious ending of *Huckleberry Finn*.

Mark Twain was characteristically fond of a photograph of himself whose effect turns on a trick, not in the taking of it but on the other side of the darkroom wall—a chance freak of chemistry. The photographer, a Mr. T. B. Hyde, thought this Jekyll effect "spoiled" the picture, but when Mark Twain saw it, "he was extravagant in his praise and had a great number of post cards printed from it. The background is all mottled," explained Hyde, "as I forgot to add the methol to the developer. When no picture appeared I suddenly remembered it had been omitted. When I did add it the crystals settled on the plate, causing the mottled appearance. Mark Twain thought it 'tapestry-like.' " In his admiration the author mingled his characteristic vanity and his love of gadgetry, the childlike awe of processes that he often harnessed to his greed for profit. One wonders if he thought of patenting Hyde's mistake. One imagines he did:

A CHINA MUG

155

Dorothy Quick remembered that when she posed as an Indian princess, Mark Twain wished aloud "that there was such a thing as color photography so that those rich reds and that heavenly shade of turquoise blue need not be lost." The colors were later supplied by having the photograph tinted, but, according to Dorothy, Mark Twain predicted that "some day they will have color photography." As a matter of of fact, they already did, and it was not long before Mark Twain and technology once again converged. In December of 1908, Alvin Langdon Coburn took a number of Lumière Autotype plates, two of which decorate Henderson's book, and in that same month a New York photographer, William Ireland Starr, made, according to Mark Twain's own remarks in the Stormfield guest book, "the colored photographs of Margaret & me that I prize so much." This was Margaret Blackmer, one of the Angel Fish, but the pictures of her and Mark Twain, along with most of Coburn's plates, have gone the way of much that is glass.

But Starr also took a series of stereoscopic slides, which have survived, and which not only convey the illusion of life but strikingly illustrate the closing chapter of Mark Twain's life, being arrangements that demonstrate the whole matter of chance.

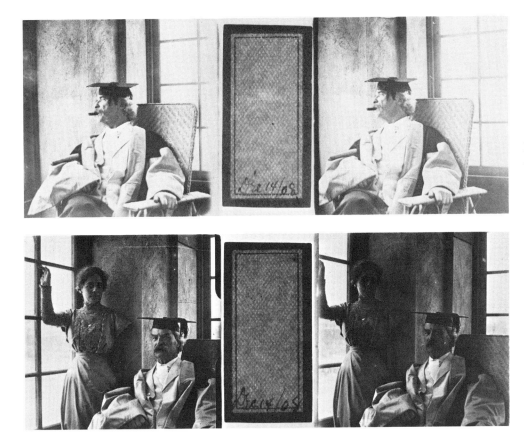

Posed alone,
with cigar
and Oxford gown,

then with Isabel,

157

and with Isabel and Ralph Ashcroft—a composition calculated to increase the illusion of depth—Mark Twain is the central object in a somewhat sinister masque, the mood of which depends on the viewer's knowledge of what was happening when they were taken, late in 1908. A gloss on the last composition is provided by Isabel, who took advantage of the occasion to take a picture of her own, casting a strong shadow on the wall, not unlike the silhouettes left by victims of other explosions. We may compare this picture with one taken of Jean at Upton House by Albert Paine, in which the shadows seem to be a conscious comment on her tragic fate, not known of course in 1906 but surely anticipated.

The total effect of all this camera work is to blur beyond definition the borderline between art and document so far as the facts of Mark Twain's last years are concerned. What was true of his autobiographical fiction and his fictional autobiography is equally true of the photographic record, part and parcel of the tendency of Mark Twain's life—and the lives of those around him—to assume recognizable patterns of circumstantial plot. Never more than a careless, haphazard writer, willing to stuff a fabric to the bursting point in order to pile up wordage, Mark Twain himself becomes in the end a central figure in alternative dramas à la Shakespeare or Henry James. Whether viewed as a tragedy or a comedy, the events of his last years are most certainly a story that few surviving photographs can illustrate, save indirectly. The photographs serve instead as ironic contrast, either supporting Paine's glorified version or pointing up Isabel's misplaced devotion. Yet they also illustrate the life-in-art and art-in-life motif, being a projection of the old man's ego—whether in terms of tableau or single images—though one that is often belied by the final effect. As in so much with which he was involved, Mark Twain in pictures conveys the most when attempting the least, and the greatest effects are often those not intended.

Thimble Theatre

CHAPTER 16

In considering Mark Twain on film, we must always remember, as those who knew him testified, that he was a consummate actor who even in undress remained on stage. In reading Paine's biography, which relies heavily on Mark Twain's improved version of his past, one is reminded of the purportedly intimate record of the last days of another master showman, megalomaniac, and master of southwestern vernacular prose (and dirty jokes), for like Lyndon B. Johnson, Mark Twain knew how to stage-manage his own dramas. Dorothy

Quick had lively memories of Mark Twain playing charades at Stormfield, and in her opinion "the stage lost a great artist when Mark Twain turned to letters," a polite way of saying he was an incurable (though well-smoked) ham. He is seldom caught off-guard by Isabel's candid camera, and many of her pictures (like Paine's) are of a man self-consciously posed, even in this series of Mark Twain strolling in his favorite costume along a woodland path.

164

It was Mark Twain who arranged Paine's Copley House photographs into a little monologue, making a playlet out of an otherwise random series of shots, and this dramatic aspect is dominant in a number of sequences taken by Isabel Lyon—perhaps inspired by the motion picture made at Stormfield. As in the series above the result resembles stills from a movie, a similarity most striking

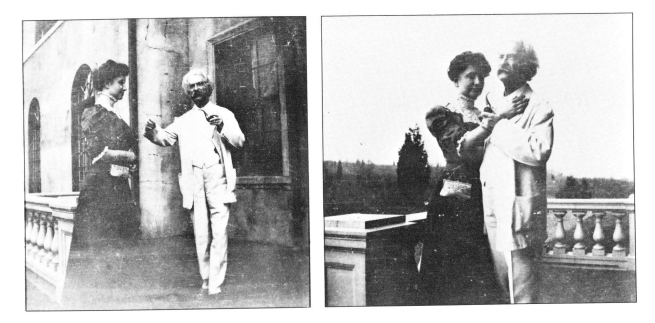

in a sequence taken by Miss Lyon of the arrival at Stormfield of Helen Keller, a
brief scenario or newsreel filled with the sentimental tensions of the day and
tight with Mark Twain's self-conscious presence. By contrast, Miss Keller remains at ease, her insouciance given a certain poignance by the situation, for
despite her genius at overcoming the handicaps of blindness and deafness, she
was separated forever from the world on film.

167

Another sequence by Isabel Lyon is of Mark Twain on shipboard, presumably bound for (or from) Bermuda. Here he is relaxing against the rail in one of his comic hats.

Now he seems to be straightening his tie in preparation for

Here he is, having the catch recorded, proud as Ernest Hemingway with one of his prow-nosed mackerel,

encountering the Angel Fish he has now captured.

and then we are on location in Bermuda,

Isabel Lyon on Mark Twain's left.

Next we have a sequence in which Mark Twain shares the blue waters of the Atlantic with Helen Allen, one of the more reluctant members of the Aquarium, a series unequaled in the annals of famous American writers on film. An absolute antidote to the sanitized poses selected and approved for Elizabeth Wallace's *Happy Island,* it nonetheless features a very clean old man. And yet, viewing the old buck in the water with his Angel Fish, it is hard not to recall his Neckar fantasy, a subliminal thought that as a very short subject brings us to the last of the Bermuda movies.

Unlike the Helen Keller and shipboard and surfside scenarios, what follows is probably not an intentional collaboration. These pictures are but a few of many taken during this period, and the ones of Dorothy Quick were taken in a different place. Yet obedient to the laws of chance, they fall together like crystals solidifying out of liquid chemicals, the kind of circumstances that contain the secret of life. Providing a pattern familiar to a viewer acquainted with Mark Twain's life and work, the plot is not for once the work of the author, and unlike all the sequences that have come earlier, it is a truly candid production. There is the white suit, the outlandish Oxford robes, the little girl in arch and not always successful (but entirely subordinate) postures, and the omnipresent Bermuda background. But as an action it takes the direction we associate with Huckleberry Finn, dominated by the motif of flight—of repudiation—here enacted by the man who starred in so many of Mark Twain's books, at last merged in an apotheotic finale with the identity of his greatest creation.

Like Huck, he puts behind him the sentimental images of a cloying, clinging, woman-ridden civilization, fleeing the shore for the freedom and joy of life afloat. In his derby hat and with a crazy umbrella, he is also a forevision of the forever fleeing Charlie Chaplin, much as a tramp is one of the chief characters in his last fragmentary fictions, through whose bloodstream moves a person named "Huck." This is finally the Mark Twain that counts, raffish, picaresque, and in motion, an old rascal cut loose at last, and roaring at the joke, the stub of a dying cigar in his mouth, hell-bent but bound for glory still. Let us leave him there, not in his coffin but with Huck Finn adrift and moving on, like his Captain Stormfield astride a meteor and heading for eternity, toward a growing sound of laughter as the earth spins far beyond all mortal care.

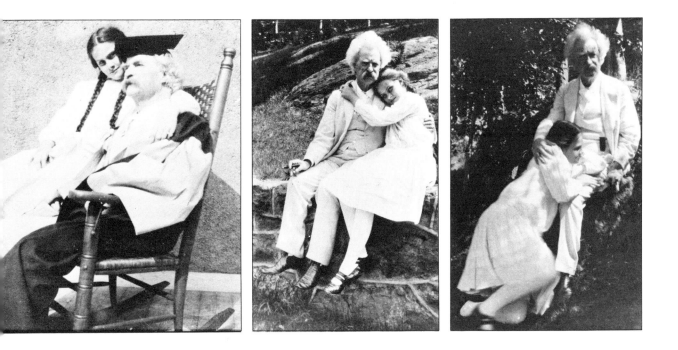

BIBLIOGRAPHY

Brooks, Van Wyck. *The Ordeal of Mark Twain.* New York: Dutton, 1920.

Clemens, Samuel L. *The Autobiography of Mark Twain: Including Chapters Now Published for the First Time.* Edited by Charles Neider. New York: Harper & Brothers, 1959.

———. *Mark Twain in Eruption: Hitherto Unpublished Pages About Men and Events.* Edited by Bernard De Voto. New York: Harper & Brothers, 1940.

———. *Mark Twain's Notebooks & Journals.* Vols. I & II (1855–1883). Edited by Frederick Anderson *et al.* Berkeley: University of California Press, 1975.

———. *The Writings of Mark Twain.* Stormfield Edition. 38 vols. New York: Harper & Brothers, 1929.

Clemens, Samuel L., and Howells, William Dean. *Mark Twain–Howells Letters: The Correspondence of Samuel L. Clemens and William D. Howells, 1872–1910.* Edited by Henry Nash Smith and William Gibson with the assistance of Frederick Anderson. 2 vols. Cambridge, Mass.: Harvard University Press, 1960.

Greenslet, Ferris. *Thomas Bailey Aldrich.* Boston: Houghton Mifflin, 1928.

Harkins, E. F. *Famous Authors (Men).* Boston: L. C. Page, 1901.

Henderson, Archibald. *Mark Twain.* New York: Frederick A. Stokes, 1910.

Hill, Hamlin. *Mark Twain: God's Fool.* New York: Harper & Row, 1973.

Howells, William Dean. *My Mark Twain.* New York: Harper & Brothers, 1910.

Jensen, Pennfield. "Mark Twain." *California Monthly,* vol. 87, no. 1 (October 1976).

Kaplan, Justin. *Mr. Clemens and Mark Twain: A Biography.* New York: Simon and Schuster, 1966.

Legman, Gershon. "Another Side of Twain." *Bookletter,* vol. 3, no. 8 (December 6, 1976).

Meltzer, Milton. *Mark Twain Himself.* New York: Bonanza Books, 1960.

Paine, Albert Bigelow. *Mark Twain: A Biography.* 4 vols. New York: Harper & Brothers, 1912.

Quick, Dorothy. *Enchantment: A Little Girl's Friendship with Mark Twain.* Norman: University of Oklahoma Press, 1961.

Salsbury, Edith Colgate, ed. *Susy and Mark Twain: Family Dialogues.* New York: Harper & Row, 1965.

Wallace, Elizabeth. *Mark Twain and The Happy Island.* Chicago: A. C. McClurg, 1913.